The Complete Guide to Spring Training 2017 / Arizona

THE COMPLETE GUIDE TO SPRING TRAINING 2017 / ARIZONA

Kevin Reichard

Lineup Books / August Publications
Middleton, WI

CONTENTS

The Complete Guide to Spring Training 2017 / Arizona

August Publications
7600 Terrace Av., Suite 204
Middleton, WI 53562
608.836.3730
augustpublications.com

ISBN 978-1-938532-29-0

9 8 7 6 5 4 3 2 1

Designer (cover): Natalie Nowytski

WARM BREEZES, COLD BEER, SUNNY SKIES

*People ask me what I do in the winter when there's no baseball.
I'll tell you what I do. I stare out the window and wait for spring.*
–Rogers Hornsby

Spring training is America's annual transformation from darkness
to light, from cold to warm, when millions of baseball fans—both
hardcore and casual—descend upon warmer climes to shed their

winter blues. For those of us living north of the Mason-Dixon line, baseball's spring training is not a luxury but a necessity, our reward for living in climates filled with overcast skies, snow, ice, and rain.

Beer and brats in hand, we arrive at Arizona spring-training games every March to soak up some sun and catch some baseball. We wait months for that first whiff of freshly mown grass at the ballpark, that first foul ball, that first inevitable sunburn. Who cares whether the starting pitcher is some kid who will likely begin the season in Double-A Tulsa? As long as the drinks are cold and the dogs are hot, all is right with the world.

We begin planning our winter getaways months in advance, juggling airline schedules and hotel openings to ensure the maximum number of games. We show up to morning workouts, just to stand by the fences and feel like we're part of the action. And we take spring-training performances a lot more seriously than do the players and managers.

This book is both for the hardcore baseball fan going to spring training to scout out their favorite team in depth, and the more casual fan who heads to spring training more in search of the perfect suntan than in search of this year's spring phenom. In fact, the casual fan is more likely to get something out of this book. While the hardcores just want to know the shortest route between their hotel and the ballpark, the casual fan knows that the richness of spring training is augmented with visits to local restaurants, shopping areas, and area attractions.

Spring training in Arizona is a concentrated affair, where 15 teams train in the greater Phoenix area at just 10 facilities. This concentration makes for baseball nirvana, as you can hit a large number of games with relatively little fuss. A spring-training game in Tempe or Peoria tends to be a rowdier affair, with kids romping through the outfield berm and college kids letting off some steam. Florida is your father's spring training, and Arizona is a party.

We've arranged this book by ballpark, in alphabetical order: Camelback Ranch at Glendale (Chicago White Sox, Los Angeles Dodgers), Sloan Park (Chicago Cubs), Goodyear Ballpark (Cincinnati Reds, Cleveland Indians), Hohokam Stadium (Oakland Athletics), Maryvale Baseball Park (Milwaukee Brewers), Peoria Stadium (San Diego Padres, Seattle Mariners), Salt River Fields at Talking Stick (Arizona Diamondbacks, Colorado Rockies), Scotts-dale Stadium (San Francisco Giants), Surprise Stadium (Kansas City Royals, Texas Rangers), and Tempe Diablo Stadium (Los Angeles Angels of Anaheim). We additionally include information about Las Vegas's Cashman Field, where games could also be held in March, as well as college facilities in both Phoenix and Tucson.

Finally, a word or two of warning. When it comes to restaurants and attractions, things can change quickly. The listings here were current as of October 2016, but it would not be surprising if a restaurant listed in this book went out of business, or if there were other changes between publication and the time you read this book. The same holds true with regard to the spring-training ball-parks and events. When in doubt, check this book's Website, **springtrainingonline.com**, for up-to-the-minute information.

ACKNOWLEDGEMENTS

Welcome to the 2017 version of **The Complete Guide to Spring Training**—the Arizona edition geared toward the Cactus League in the Valley of the Sun. This is the sixth edition of the book, and we're just as excited about spring training as we were a decade ago, when the first edition appeared.

Originally we conceived of **The Complete Guide to Spring Training** as a book covering spring training both in Arizona and Florida. We knew most baseball fans weren't going to hit spring training in both states, but there was plenty of information applicable to both states, and the logistics of book publishing required us to offer a single printed work.

Now, in this brave new world of publishing, we're freed from so many of these seemingly arbitrary shackles. The rise of eBooks and on-demand printing meant we could overhaul our approach and split our coverage between two state-specific guides. You're holding an edition specific for your state, and we were able to boost the amount of content accordingly.

This book didn't occur in a vacuum. Thanks go to the readers of Spring Training Online, the Internet gathering spot for true spring-training fans. It's an amazingly passionate and fascinating community—a continual delight.

Thanks to my family: my wife, Courtney, and my kids, Sean, Rachel, and Sarah, who find themselves being dragged to every manner of ballpark, big and small, all spring and summer long.

Most of all, thanks to the loyal readers of Ballpark Digest, a website I launched in the side in July 2002, that has blossomed into a full-time job. Not everyone can turn their passion into their career, and I'm lucky enough to say I've done so.

—Kevin Reichard
October 2016

SPRING TRAINING: AN AMERICAN TRADITION

We live in an increasingly crowded sports marketplace, but one thing remains constant: the appeal of low-tech, low-stress spring training, a time considered by many to be the best time in the baseball season. While the grandstands aren't wooden anymore and there are few pitchers doing wind sprints in the outfield, spring training is still a celebration of everything that is right with baseball.

Spring training has remained a cornerstone activity for baseball fans hardcore and casual, though it has certainly changed over the years. In the not-too-distant past, spring training could be attended on a whim, with plenty of good seats available at the gate and fewer than a thousand fans in the stands. Those days are long gone and, in this age of fans seeking great experiences of all sorts, spring training has exploded in popularity over the last 20 years.

How popular is spring training? In 2015, the Cactus League attracted over 2 million fans attending games, and in previous years it was estimated spring training generated some $632 million in year-around economic activity in the greater Phoenix area. That level of economic activity is impressive considering Arizona is an area that's not necessarily synonymous with spring breaks and spending.

Though the beginning of spring training marks the official start of the baseball season, teams prepare for training camp months in advance. Planning starts at the end of the prior season, when team equipment managers start laying in supplies in advance of spring training, and team officials begin mapping out spring-training schedules.

In fact, Truck Day is now regarded by many as the unofficial launch to spring training: in early February each team will ship its equipment from the home ballpark to the spring-training site. We're talking some serious baggage here: the Oakland A's send 22,000 pounds of equipment to Phoenix and ship 30,000 pounds back to Oakland.

Spring training now requires a certain level of planning from fans as well: timeshares and hotels must be reserved, relatives must be warned, vacations must be requested, and school schedules must be consulted. We understand. It can be difficult at times to plan for spring training, as schedules are usually released well after the

World Series. In this chapter, we'll go through the steps needed to prepare for your spring travels.

This book doesn't have any schedules. We're still a month or two before unofficial schedules are released, and several months before MLB releases official schedules in the middle of January 2017. And that January date may not be the final drop-down date: in 2016, there were more changes at the end of January and early February, when the schedules were still being changed to accommodate a Tampa Bay Rays game in Cuba. At all times you can catch schedules both permanent and tentative at **springtrainingonline.com**.

INSIDER'S TIP
We do a Spring Training Online newsletter, and we send out issues when schedules are updated. It's free, and you can sign up at **springtrainingonline.com**.

This year's spring-training schedule will be different than in past years, as the World Baseball Classic is slated for 2017. That means some players will be reporting a little earlier to camps, with more off dates to accommodate World Baseball Classic games. In 2016, teams began to report to spring training on Feb. 17, and spring training games began on Feb. 28. Games should begin around Feb. 24 or so—several days earlier than in past years.

Now, that can be a plus or minus for you. By and large, the World Baseball Classic is an event run outside the auspices of spring training: in 2013, during the previous WBC, only one spring-training venue (Salt River Fields at Talking Stick) was used for WBC games. None are slated to be used for 2017. However, some WBC squads will be training at spring-training camps, so you may unexpectedly see a star training out on a practice field, and national teams will be taking on MLB teams in exhibitions. We'll be monitoring the WBC at the **springtrainingonline.com** site, and we will pass along both venue and practice information as it becomes available.

Planning Your Trip

There are three ways to approach a visit to spring training: for games, for workouts, or for both. We love doing both—workouts in the morning, a game in the afternoon—but there are plenty of folks who focus on games as their spring-training experience.

For many, their spring training begins when it does for players: on reporting day. Typically players report to spring training around Valentine's Day, with pitchers and catchers reporting first. (As we know from the previous section, however, this date may be moved up a little to accommodate World Baseball Classic schedules.) Decades ago, that first reporting day was a big deal: Players were reentering the baseball world from their offseason jobs, and they were subject to a physical, a weigh-in, and a general evaluation by team officials. With players mostly out of touch between November and February, there were always some surprises on reporting day.

For today's baseball player, the game is a full-time job. Virtually every player trains in the offseason or plays winter ball, and organizations keep fairly close tabs on most players, especially the well-paid prospects and superstars. There are very few surprises come that first reporting date, as many players have already been hanging out around training facilities for several weeks or months.

Many fans like to show up for those first practices. Most of these early workouts are open to the public, and they're a great way to get close to the players as they run through drills. Most practice areas are set up for fan comfort, with shaded seating and even concessions. There are some big rewards to showing up for workouts: players tend to be more accessible at those initial workouts and willing to sign autographs after practice. We cover every team's practice schedule individually; there's no uniform MLB schedule to practices, and every team sets its own start time and location. (We list them on **springtrainingonline.com**.)

INSIDER'S TIP

Practices are organized, and while MLB teams have added many creature comforts to workout facilities, they don't feel compelled to share their organization plan with you. You're welcome to observe from a respectful distance—either in the stands in the main ballpark or somewhere next to the practice field—and teams are very explicit about where you're allowed to watch. Many teams rope off access to specific areas of the training complex at certain times. At the end of the day, the attitude from many MLB teams is that practices are for players, not for fans.

Games begin Feb. 24-Feb. 25 (as of now) and run through the last weekend of March, and it's then the practice schedule changes. Most teams will gather in the morning for workouts, but the real focus is the afternoon game. You can show up early and see who you can catch at the morning workout. (Indeed, that's one of the big advantages of a modern spring facility like Camelback Ranch-Glendale or Salt River Fields: they are designed to bring fans close to practice areas before they ever hit the ballpark.) Conversely, if a team is on the road, the regulars not scheduled for the trip will work out in the morning during a regularly scheduled workout time.

In fact, this emphasis on games versus long workouts designed to sweat the booze out of out-of-shape players is perhaps the biggest shift in the modern age of spring training. Most players come to spring training in shape, so the need for intense physical workouts is mitigated. Most teams have their rosters set weeks before spring training: in this age of guaranteed contracts and high-priced players, only a handful of roster spots are at stake on the average MLB squad. It's not like the old days where a player could legitimately win a starting spot in spring camp. Sure, there's always competition, and occasionally a phenom will win a starting spot in spring training, but by and large most MLB managers can pencil in their starting lineups before spring training begins. The competitions, really, are for the last few spots on a roster: the last two pitchers in the bullpen, the fifth outfielder should a team carry five, the backup catcher, etc.

So why go to practices? Eagerness to begin the season. Enthusiasm for the upcoming campaign. Desire to snare an autograph.

Though you'll find plenty of fans milling around camp after players report, the real action starts when games begin at the end of February and early March. This, for most fans, is the real beginning of spring training. And although the starting lineups during those first few weeks of games will bear little resemblance to the Opening Day lineup, enough stars will be present to make those games worthwhile. In general, you'll need a long lineup card to keep track of all the players shuttling on and off the field for those games: pitchers are restricted by pitch and inning counts; starters are limited to just three or four innings on the field, and by the seventh inning you'll be watching mostly players already ticketed for time at the Triple-A or Double-A levels.

So what? You're out in the sun at a glorious time of year partaking in America's Pastime. It's a great experience no matter if you're watching a starting MLB pitcher or a kid destined (in the short-term, at least) to be an Arkansas Traveler.

One more thing to note when scheduling your time: most spring-training games are played in the afternoon. Some teams do not schedule any night games; others will schedule several. In the Cactus League, any night game is a bonus. The relatively short distances between ballparks assures that a hardcore spring-training fan can easily take in two games in one day, and with Arizona State University playing a full slate of night games at Phoenix

Municipal Stadium, it's very easy to set up a day-night double-header.

How to Order Tickets

There's no one date when all MLB teams put spring-training tickets on sale: each team sets a sale date separately, sometimes with very little warning. (To wit: In the very recent past the Tampa Bay Rays announced on a Monday that tickets would be going on sale the following Friday. In 2011 and 2012 the Boston Red Sox didn't even bother to pre-announce tickets were on sale: tickets went on sale right after the press release was issued. Didn't matter; the Red Sox sold every spring-training ticket within hours.) No team has put tickets on sale yet.

Unless you are lucky enough to score tickets when they go on sale, you'll need to order them from teams—and deal with the distinct possibility that popular games are sold out or the better seats are already snared—or deal with the resale market.

Buying your ticket directly from the team will usually be the cheapest way to snare a ducat. With popular teams, the selection will be limited. Every team sells spring season tickets, bought mostly by locals and snowbirds, and the best tickets in any spring ballpark are controlled by these season-ticket holders.

Still, tickets are available from a variety of sources. Most people assume that only MLB teams sell tickets, but that's not the case. MLB does sell the majority of spring-training tickets, but there are usually some alternative ways to come up with ducats for a popular match.

For sheer convenience, however, your search for tickets should begin with the MLB teams. They're set up best to sell massive amounts of tickets in a short amount of time; the beginning of spring-training ticket sales can best be described as a feeding frenzy, as tens of thousands of fans rush to obtain tickets for specific games.

There are four ways to order spring-training tickets directly from MLB teams: via telephone, via the Internet, in person, and via the U.S. Mail. We'll describe each.

- **Via telephone**. Most tickets are sold via phone sales. This can be a frustrating way of doing things, as you're likely to encounter some busy signals or long wait times when tickets first go on sale. Don't bother calling before the tickets are technically on sale: all you'll do is waste your time and irritate the ticket reps. They can't help you until the tickets are actually on sale; they won't call you back, and they won't put you on a secret list to be hauled out when tickets are on sale. When the tickets do go on sale, be prepared to call early in the day for popular games, like the A's-Giants matchups. You'll also pay a "ticketing fee" for the convenience of buying tickets.
- **Via the Internet**. Every team sells spring-training tickets via the Internet. There are some pluses and minuses to this approach. On the one hand, you can bypass clogged phone lines and make your purchases directly (although Ticketmaster has implemented the equivalent of telephone wait times when you buy popular tickets online). New ticketing systems are sophisticated: many teams have systems where you can order specific seats or see a list of available seats within a section and select the ones you want. And yes, you'll also pay a ticketing fee for the convenience of buying tickets.
- **In person**: Most teams sell spring-training tickets at their main ticket office at the major-league ballpark, the spring-training ticket office, or local team stores. The Colorado Rockies, for example, sell spring-training

tickets at the Denver-area Rockies Dugout Stores. There
are three big advantages to buying tickets in person: you
can usually get a good idea of the range of available
tickets, you can request specific seats, and you won't
need to wait too long in line. Plus, the major-league and
spring-training box offices are the only locations where
you won't incur handling fees.

- **Via U.S. Mail**. Some teams sell tickets via the mail. You
  send in your money for a certain price range, and you
  take whatever tickets the team decides to send you. Will
  you receive the best tickets in your price range?
  Depends on the whims of a ticket rep with the team. The
  advantage, however, is that these orders tend to be filled
  first, so you are virtually assured of receiving tickets to
  the game of your choice. Not every team offers this
  service.

INSIDER'S TIP

If you order tickets and plan on picking them up at the ballpark, make sure you have the confirmation number and an
ID with you. Ticket-office personnel are instructed to make
sure that the right person is picking up tickets. More than
once have we waited in the Will Call line and cooled our
heels while the party in front of us argues in vain with the
ticket staff over disputed tickets.

Teams also offer two more ways to obtain tickets that may fit your
needs.

If you think you'll be attending many games, consider a season
ticket. Season-ticket packages go on sale weeks before single-
game tickets; usually season tickets are the province of locals and
brokers, but if you really, really want some tix for the Athletics-
Giants games and realize that you have no chance of obtaining a
good ticket via conventional means, spring for the season ticket

and then try and sell tickets to some of the other games via eBay or StubHub.

Other teams offer a break to groups of 10 or more. Again, this won't apply if just you and your buddies are in a group, but there may be opportunities where you could put together a group (via a church organization, an Internet chat site, etc.) that could buy discounted tickets to a game or two. These transactions require some interaction with a sales agent: at this time no team is offering discounted group tickets online.

INSIDER'S TIP

If you can, schedule a game on St. Patrick's Day. It's the only real holiday in the month, and most teams do something to commemorate it, whether it be cheap green beer, green uniforms, or the giveaway of something green. You can also bet watering holes close to the ballparks will have some St. Patrick's Day drink specials as well.

Working with Brokers

There is another way to obtain a single-game ticket: through a ticket broker. This is indeed American capitalism at its finest: good brokers tend to have decent tickets to the best games. They also put tickets on sale early, giving you peace of mind in your planning process. They're also not shy about telling the world about the availability of the tickets, so if you want to go to a game badly enough, chances are good one of them will step up with a ticket. (The newest trend in the broker world: like teams, they offer downloadable etickets.) We work with a very reputable vendor to offer tickets at **ballparkdigesttickets.com**; of course, we'd recommend you start there.

Where to Stay

If you lack friends or family in Arizona, you'll need to arrange housing for your stay. There are a few ways to go.

The obvious choice is a hotel. Every spring-training site in the Phoenix area is located in an urban or suburban area and features easy access to a slew of hotels. You'll pay more to stay near the more popular ballparks; in our guides to each venue we list the closest hotels to each ballpark and tell you if it's worth staying near the ballpark. (In many cases, it's not.) There are some base-ball fanatics who insist on staying within walking distance of a spring-training facility, but they a) tend to spend the entire day at the facility and b) don't want to spring for the cost of a car.

In the chapters covering specific complexes, we list the local num-bers for hotels located close to the ballparks, as well as the official hotel for every team. Yes, fans—not just baseball Annies—still hang around hotel lobbies hoping for a glimpse of a star or a potential autograph opportunity. You won't be alone.

Only in rare situations will you be shut out of an affordable hotel room for spring training—provided that you can be flexible about where you stay. There are many hotels in Scottsdale catering to the spring-training fan, and there are also hotels near Sky Harbor catering to business travelers. Past that, hotels tend to be scattered throughout the Valley, but usually located near some major inter-state interchange. Given the intimate nature of spring training in the Valley of the Sun, unless you end up in the far reaches of the market, you're never going to be too far away from any spring-training venue. Granted, there are some caveats—if you're a Texas Rangers or Kansas City Royals fan, you probably don't want to stay out in Chandler or Apache Junction—but you'll probably find plenty of hotel rooms in the northwest quadrant of the Valley, in any case: in recent years we've seen a lot of new hotels opening in the Peoria/Glendale/Surprise area.

You can also investigate a package deal involving a hotel. Most teams and many hotels now offer package deals, which combine a hotel stay with tickets to a game or two.

But there are some alternatives to daily-stay hotels. The most prominent is a residence-sharing service like Airbnb or VRBO, where you can see the specifics of the rental before committing. There are plenty of listings for the likes of Phoenix or Scottsdale during spring training. While they may not be the cheapest venues under the sun, you won't get that hotel feel when staying at someone else's residence. Depending on your viewpoint, that's either a good thing or a bad thing.

If you're planning on an extended stay, consider renting a condo or RV. Almost every area listed in the book has condos or time-shares for rent. We've not going to delve heavily into the topic, but there are places in this book where we note the availability of condos or timeshares.

There are many folks who visit spring training in the comfort of their own RV; they're the ones setting up shop three or four hours before a game, grilling their pregame brats, and watching the noontime news. Though you can't park overnight at a ballpark parking lot, most communities hosting spring training also have several RV parks, and some ballparks, like the one in Peoria, have special areas set up for RV parking. The greater Phoenix market is geared toward snowbirds, and snowbirds like RVs; hence the need for RV parks. We note them throughout this book.

You don't even need to own an RV to use one for spring training: Companies like Cruise America rent RVs by the day or week from hundreds of locations across the United States. Today's RV is not like yesterday's RV: they have considerably more amenities (like showers, decent bathrooms, and air conditioning) and are more reliable than in the past. And RV parks can be amazingly upscale, with shaded parking, wireless networking, and more.

Making Your Way to the Ballpark: Planes, Trains, and Automobiles

Getting to the city hosting spring training is one thing. Making your way to your hotel room and the ballpark is another.

While public transit has improved in Phoenix thanks to light rail, the transit system really isn't geared to spring-training fans. (Light rail, alas, doesn't serve a single spring-training facility, although there is talk about extending a line to Sloan Park in the future.) Yes, you can rely on buses to get to many facilities, and *valleymetro.org* lists all the light-rail and bus schedules and routes. But, realistically, unless you're staying at a hotel within walking distance of a ballpark that is also adjacent to plenty of dining and shopping options (i.e., hello, downtown Scottsdale!), you'll need to resign yourself to an inevitable cost of attending spring training: springing for a car. Sure, you could drive your own car to spring training—and trust us, plenty of folks do just that, as evidenced by the large number of Colorado license plates in the Salt River Fields parking lot throughout March—but if you're committed to flying, you're going to be forced to rent a car.

Luckily for you, rental cars are plentiful in Arizona. Alas, they are expensive and highly taxed.

> **INSIDER'S TIP**
> There are no car rentals at Sky Harbor. They were all relocated several years ago to an offsite facility. This is more convenient than it sounds: shuttles run every few minutes from the airport to the facility, and it's easy to get in and out of there. Just be sure to factor in this when you're planning your return trip: add 25 minutes to give yourself enough time to return the car and take the shuttle to the airport.

> **INSIDER'S TIP**
> Consider an alternative to rental cars: ridesharing services

like Uber and Lyft. The appeal: you can order a car at a specific place at a specific time, and you can be dropped off at or near the ballpark. (Most, but not every spring-training ballpark has a designated dropoff area. But any smart driver in Peoria or Scottsdale can get you fairly close to the ballpark.) They definitely lessen the need for a rental car for those staying in more urban areas, like Scottsdale or Peoria: you could certainly stay at a neighborhood hotel and then arrange a rideshare to and from the games.

Attending a Game: Some General Guidelines

Now that you actually have a game ticket, a plane ticket, a hotel room, and a car, you're all ready to actually attend a spring-training game. Congratulations!

There are some things you should know.

- Most spring-training ballparks open at least two hours before game time, and they generally run the same schedule for a 1:05 p.m. game start, which we note on team pages. (Alas, there's no uniform MLB schedule for when workouts start.) This is usually the best time to score autographs: players are relaxed during their warm-ups and happy to wander over to the stands and sign away. Or you could head to the practice facility in the morning and try to score some autographs there. Newer spring-training complexes, like Salt River Fields and Camelback Ranch-Glendale, put a premium on player accessibility. They're built to give you a chance to get up close and personal with players and coaches in a very pleasant atmosphere.

• Many of the ushers at spring-training games are volunteers, usually seniors living in the area. Don't hassle them: they're volunteering at games because they love baseball. Some of them can be a little on the officious side, but remember their job is to make sure fans are in their proper seats. In Peoria, 581 "Diamond Backers" in the Peoria Diamond Club work Seattle and San Diego games as ushers, program sellers, parking-lot attendants, and more. In Surprise, the Sundancers help out with game-day operations.

• You're not always assured of seeing a superstar or even a famous player at a spring-training game. Teams are notorious for leaving their best players at home. There is a rule that each team must send four regulars on the road to play in an exhibition game, but there's a big difference between a superstar and a regular on most teams.

• Don't be in a hurry to leave the ballpark once a game is done. Some coaches will hold a practice right after an afternoon game, either in the main ballpark or a practice field. This doesn't happen as often as it once did, unfortunately. Another bonus to remaining for entire games: players will usually sign on their way back to the clubhouses.

- If you're lucky, you'll see pitchers indulging in one of the great old traditions of spring training: running outfield wind sprints in the midst of a game. Back in the day teams trained under extremely limited circumstances: one big playing field and one small clubhouse was enough for most teams, unlike the five-field complexes used today. Because of the limited facilities and the relaxed nature of exhibition games, pitchers would run wind sprints in the outfield during games to get in shape. Of course, now that we have larger ballparks and berm seating, we don't see many pitchers run outfield wind sprints in the midst of a spring-training games. But it does happen; when it does, enjoy the moment and salute a player with an appreciation for baseball history.

"B" Games

You don't need to shell out the big bucks to see major leaguers in action during spring training.

If you're willing to put up with missing a few creature comforts like seatbacks, concessions, and restrooms, you can hit a "B" game held on a satellite field in a spring-training complex. These are pure practice games, usually held in the morning. There's no scoreboard tracking the action or an announcer announcing the players, so you should know a little about the players to get anything out of the experience.

And you can't be too much of a purist. As said, these are true practice games: players bat out of order and wander in and out of the lineup depending on the situation.

But these games are also excellent places to see the real major leaguers work on their game: you're never going to be closer to a superstar practicing one specific part of their game. Hard-working

players are legendary for using these games to work on their
swings or on specific pitches.

In the past, teams held "B" games almost daily, but they seem to
be going by the wayside. Call the team's local box office to see if
a "B" game is scheduled for a given day (they are not subject to a
published schedule), but your best bet may to be wander around a
facility in the morning and see if there's any action on a field.

Minor-League Games

Another option during your spring-training trip: taking in a minor-
league match. These games are played on satellite fields (at the
spring-training complex when possible; at a larger offsite training
facility if not) and are open to anyone wandering through the facility. Unlike "B" games, minor-league games are subject to a schedule: they begin a few weeks into spring training and feature all the
teams in an organization taking on all the teams from another
organization. For instance, the Class AAA and Class AA teams
from the Kansas City Royals will host the Class AAA and Class
AA teams from the Cleveland Indians at the satellite fields at the
Surprise Stadium training complex, while the two Class A teams
from the Indians will host the two Class A Royals teams at their
training complex next to Goodyear Ballpark. In the minors, there
are four levels of teams in training camp (AAA, AA, High A and
Low A); if the AAA and AA teams are home, the A teams will be
away, and vice versa. Again, these games are run on a casual
basis, and most of the better players will be with the parent team,
but they offer a very intimate view of some of tomorrow's superstars. Schedules for these games are released after the beginning of
the year; check **springtrainingonline.com** for a complete list of
minor-league schedules.

Weather

You can tell a spring-training rookie by their beet-red face and sunburned shoulders. If you've spent the last four months cooped up in a climate dominated by snow and ice, you're likely to do the logical thing and bask for hours on end in the warm spring sun.

Don't.

Yes, you'll hear from everyone the importance of slathering on some sunscreen before hitting your first spring game. But the advice is sound: even a mildly overcast day can scorch your skin to the painful point, and you don't want to ruin your trip with a bad sunburn. Your best bet is to bring sunscreen to a spring game. If you forget, you're in luck: most Arizona spring-training facilities offer free sunscreen, usually via dispensers next to a restroom. And even if you forget and there's no free sunscreen, most team stores sell it as well. So there's no reason for you to head home with a bad sunburn.

Otherwise, you should expect good weather for your spring-training sojourn. Phoenix can still be a little chilly at night at the beginning of March, so bring a jacket for those evenings out. You can expect the weather to be sunny and warm (75 degrees or so) for most afternoon games.

What Can I Bring Into the Ballpark?

Forget about bringing much into the ballpark past a medium-sized bag. There's a uniform MLB policy regarding what you can bring into a ballpark. First, everything must fit within a backpack, cooler, or diaper bag no larger than 16 inches by 16 inches by 8 inches. Non-alcoholic beverages must be in sealed, plastic containers. Food must be stored in sealed, clear-plastic containers. If you're carrying any sort of backpack or larger bag, you will be asked to open it up for inspection. Most teams are pretty mellow about backpacks and oversized bags, even if you're bringing in some peanuts or snacks. The key is to have sealed water and food: it's a way to ensure you're not sneaking booze into the ballpark.

Unless noted otherwise, every team in this guide conforms to these MLB guidelines.

So forget about bringing a six-pack of cans or bottles into the park. You can't bring Fido or Fluffy with you unless your dog is a certified seeing-eye or service dog. And you certainly are not allowed to bring any weapons into the ballpark.

What If It Rains?

If it rains, you'll be able to exchange your ticket for a ticket to a future game; many teams also refund unused tickets in case of game cancellations due to weather. You will not be refunded any service or parking.

A SHORT HISTORY OF SPRING TRAINING

Brooklyn Dodgers training in Hot Springs, Arkansas, 1912. (Library of Congress)

Spring training has been around almost as long as professional baseball. The best evidence points to spring training first taking place in 1870, when the Cincinnati Red Stockings and the Chicago White Stockings held organized baseball camps in New Orleans. By 1886, spring training had spread throughout professional baseball, with at least four professional teams holding a formal training camp, and *The Sporting News* lauding the development in its inaugural March 17, 1886, issue:

The preparatory work now being done by two or three
prominent clubs in the country marks one of the most
sensible departures from the old rut in base-ball that has
ever been made. It has always been a matter of wonder to
professional and amateur athletes that men having thousands of dollars invested in a business of which so much
depends on the physical condition of their men, should
pay so little attention to the matter of training these people for the arduous work that was expected of them during the six months covering the championship season.
Take these same men and let them put the money that
they have invested in base-ball in horse-flesh. Would they
dare send their horses out on a trotting or running circuit
in the spring without training them....

Man is the superior animal and really needs more care
and attention than the horse. Yet for years ball players
have been sent out in the spring with muscles soft and
flabby, carrying from ten to twenty pounds of extra flesh,
and told to "play ball." Well, they have played ball, but
the games have been "yaller," and many a man has come
in from a first game with a shoulder, a leg or an arm that
has impaired his effectiveness for an entire season....

That season saw the Chicago White Stockings go to Hot Springs,
Ark., for spring training, while the Philadelphia Phillies headed for
Charleston, S.C., for some games against local talent. The White
Stockings were owned and managed by A.G. Spalding (the same
Spalding who founded the sporting-goods firm that exists to this
day), who told *The Sporting News* of his plans to literally "boil"
the members of his team in Hot Springs for two weeks:

"It's a great scheme," said Mr. Spalding yesterday, leaning back in
his chair and stroking his forehead. "I wonder whatever made me
think of it. All the boys are enthusiastic about it and all want to go.
I have written to a professor down there, and he is making

arrangements to build a vat in which he can boil the whole nine at once....I boil out all the alcoholic microbes which may have impregnated the systems of these men during the winter while they have been away from me and Anson....If that don't work I'll send 'em all over to Paris and have 'em inoculated by Pasteur."

By 1900, spring training was firmly established as a baseball ritual, with most American and National League teams heading out of town so players could train (i.e., dry out) and managers could evaluate. In those days, spring training was a considerably looser affair: players would gather in a Florida, California, Texas, Arkansas, or Louisiana city, work out for several days, sweat out the winter booze, perhaps sample some of the local delights (many teams held spring training in Hot Springs, with the city's notable gambling establishments as an inducement to report), and then make their way back to their homes while barnstorming daily against local teams.

Even so, spring training was never a strenuous activity in the past. Take the Cleveland Indians of the 1920s, who trained in Lakeland at a ballpark still standing, Henley Field. Most teams worked out only once a day, either for an hour or two; the rest of the time the players were free to play golf and carouse—which many of them did. In the 1924 *Reach Guide*, Jack Ryder reported that Indians manager Tris Speaker was a firm believer in a single, brief but intense daily workout.

Other teams of that era were more intense. The Brooklyn Dodgers were known for their three-hour workouts, while Pat Moran, manager of the Cincinnati Reds, held 10 a.m. and 2 p.m. workouts. Ryder seemed to approve of the Reds' schedule:

> It is the observation of this writer that the policy of Manager Moran is the best of those outlined. Ball players are young men, many of them merely boys, full of pepper and anxious to work. They all enjoy the spring training after the long lay-

off of the winter. They do not ask to coddled or favored with light labor. In fact, the more work they can get, provided it is not up to the point of exhaustion, the better they like it. Furthermore, the policy of two sessions a day of practice leaves the boys less time to themselves and keeps them together more, which is always a good thing for a team. They have less temptation to get into bad habits or bad company and the younger recruits are more apt to follow the good example set by the veterans on the team. It must not be understood that Manager Moran is a hard driver or forces his players too far, quite the reverse. If he sees that any one of the athletes is lazy or inclined to shirk, he is after him at once with a sharp stick, but there are not many such cases. In most instances, the Red leader has to curb the ambition of his men instead of urging them on. This he constantly does, not allowing any man to get an inch beyond the limit of his strength.

Small Florida communities were suddenly known across the nation because of the allure provided by major-league baseball. St. Petersburg. Plant City. Orlando. Lakeland. Vero Beach. Fort Lauderdale. Sarasota. Bradenton. Tampa. Fans are dismayed these days when MLB teams look for new training facilities, but the practice is not new: since the turn of the century cities have sought to promote themselves to tourists after building spring-training facilities and guaranteeing revenues to teams. Look at the cities where the Philadelphia Athletics trained between 1903 and 1914: Jacksonville, Spartanburg (S.C.), Shreveport, Montgomery (Ala.), Dallas, New Orleans, Atlanta, San Antonio, and back to Jacksonville. No more than two years spent in a single city and whoever made the best offer to a team in January usually landed the spring training in March. That pattern prevailed until World War II.

Case in point: tiny Bogalusa, Louisiana, which hosted St. Louis Browns (the predecessor to the Baltimore Orioles) spring training in 1921. The city lured the Brownies to their fair city with the construction of a new grandstand and inexpensive accommodations at the Pine Tree Inn. The *Bogalusa Enterprise and American* of March 10, 1921 reported how pleased the Brownies were with the facilities:

> "When we ask for something at the hotel," said one of the best known players in the American League, "we are not told that 'it will be looked into,' but within a shorter time than one would expect in the best hotel in America, we are served. I never saw people so hospitable in all my life, they simply go out of their way in Bogalusa to make it enjoyable for us and I know there is not a member of the team who will not leave Bogalusa with regret when we finish our training, and I also know that if it was left to the members of the team as to where we would train next spring, that it would be Bogalusa by 100 percent."

> Manager Coleman of the Terre Haute, Ind., team of the Central League, and former manager of the Mobile club, said that the club house built here for the Browns was by far better than any club house on the American League circuit and that it passed Detroit, which had the best in the league. "The grounds," said Mr. Coleman, "are great and by next year they can be made as good as any in the country."

All of this, apparently, was not enough: the Brownies never returned to Bogalusa for spring training, heading in 1922 for Mobile, Alabama.

The first arrival of Major League Baseball in Arizona came in 1909, when the Chicago White Sox took on the local lads of Yuma while barnstorming their way back from spring training in California. In those days spring training was a completely different affair: teams would spend a few weeks at a training site and then barnstorm their way back to the Opening Day ballpark. Over the next 30 years you would have teams training in California—the

Chicago Cubs, the Pittsburgh Pirates, and the aforementioned
White Sox—stop off in Arizona to take on local teams.

The first MLB team to officially hold spring training in Arizona
was the Detroit Tigers. In 1929 the Tigers trained at Phoenix
Riverside Park and scheduled several exhibition games against
local squads. The Arizona tenure was not a success, and in 1930
the Tigers trained in California.

An early home to spring training in Phoenix was the original
Phoenix Municipal Stadium, located at Central Avenue and
Mohave Street. It was built in 1937, funded by the federal Works
Progress Administration. It hosted several levels of Minor League
Baseball—the Phoenix Senators of the old Class C Arizona-Texas
League, the Phoenix Stars of the old Class C Arizona-Mexico
League, and the original Phoenix Giants of the Class AAA Pacific
Coast League—as well as New York Yankees spring training
(1951) and New York Giants (1947-1950, 1952-1963) spring
training.

When the original Phoenix Municipal Stadium opened, Central
Avenue and Mohave Street wasn't exactly the middle of town: the
ballpark was surrounded by farmland and limited housing. This
was where the New York Giants originally trained in 1947, after
Horace Stoneham shifted spring operations from the East Coast. It
was in use until 1964, when the new Municipal Stadium opened.
(We cover it more in-depth in our chapter on Arizona State University baseball.)

Each team has a unique spring-training history, and we present
some of the highlights in each team chapter. There was one period
in spring training that bears further discussion, however: spring
training during the war years. We all associate spring training with
warmer climes, but there was a period when major-league teams
trained close to home. Travel restrictions during World War II
kept teams north of the Ohio River and east of the Mississippi

River; the St. Louis Browns and Cardinals were exempted and trained in the greater St. Louis area.

As a result, teams trained in such exotic locales as Evansville and French Lick, Ind., where both the Chicago Cubs and Chicago White Sox trained in 1943 and 1944. The East Coast teams didn't stray too far from home, either: The Brooklyn Dodgers trained at the West Point Field House between drills, and the Boston Braves trained at Choate School in Wallingford, Conn.

When the war ended, normalcy resumed—and that included baseball, which returned to springs spent mostly in Florida and Arizona. As travel and demographics changed, so did spring training. Rather than writing off spring training as a necessary expense, baseball teams saw spring training evolve into a profit center. Rather than being limited to boozy journalists and clubby insiders, spring training became open to everyone with enough money for admission.

And the reason for spring training changed as well, from a team-building exercise to a month-long advertisement. Today very few roster spots are decided in spring training, and in this era of multi-million contracts players work out in the winter, coming into camp already in shape. Very few major-league teams need six weeks to determine rosters, but spring training is so profitable and such a great advertisement for baseball that it would be impossible to scale back.

ARIZONA
AND THE
CACTUS
LEAGUE

With a concentration of complexes and 15 teams providing entertainment every day in March, Cactus League games have emerged
in recent years as one of the great sports experiences on earth.

In fact, the Cactus League set an attendance record in 2016, when
1.9 million spectators attended games in the Phoenix area. That
translated to 8,236 fans per game, with teams like the Chicago
Cubs and the San Francisco Giants playing before plenty of sell-

outs, and teams like the Los Angeles Dodgers setting attendance marks. Spring training's impact is very real: a 2015 study from Tucson-based FMR Associates estimated that Arizona spring-training ballparks generated generate more than $809 million annually—$544 from out-of-state visitors and $265 million from year-round events.

When Arizona interests lured the Giants and the Indians for spring training in 1947, spring training was a different beast in terms of economics and schedules. Teams had trained out West many times before World War II—most notably the Chicago Cubs, who first trained in Santa Monica in 1905 and then on California's Catalina Island between 1922 and 1942—and the economics were simple: owners would get some small community to subsidize spring training with direct payments and cheap or free lodging. Teams would spend a few weeks training (or drying out, in some cases), and then those ballclubs would hit the road, barnstorming their way home.

But as baseball became a big business, so did spring training. Owners were working every angle in search of more revenues, and spring training became one obvious target: with players basically working for free (salaries didn't kick in until the season started), spring training was a way to generate revenue without a lot of overhead. Barnstorming gradually gave way to longer stints at training camp; instead of traveling and playing where the fans lived, baseball teams were able to coax fans to come to them.

In fact, the early history of spring training in Arizona involves barnstorming teams. The Chicago White Sox barnstormed in 1909, stopping in Yuma for a match against a local team. Both the Cubs and White Sox made stops in Arizona during spring training for the next thirty-some years, and in 1929 the Detroit Tigers became the first team to train in Arizona, setting up residence at Riverside Park in Phoenix. Staying true to form, the Tigers played a whop-

ping two games there before barnstorming their way back to
Detroit.

The roots of the Cactus League became a reality in 1947, when
Horace Stoneham's New York Giants and Bill Veeck's Cleveland
Indians took up residence in Phoenix and Tucson, respectively.
That Veeck ended up in Tucson wasn't a surprise—he loved the
Southwest and at the time owned a ranch near Tucson. Stoneham
was a natural for Phoenix, as he was developing business interests
in the area. Stoneham went one step even further than Veeck, con-
structing a luxury development in conjunction with spring training, a route that several team owners took over the years (and are
still taking; more than one owner has floated the idea of combining a ballpark with a big-buck development). The Indians' home
was known as Randolph Baseball Park when the Indians began
training there; it was later renamed Hi Corbett Field and is now the
home of the University of Arizona Wildcats baseball program.

INSIDER'S TIP

There's a bit of romantic history surrounding the decision
by Stoneham to locate Giants spring training in Phoenix:
that he was so taken by the Buckhorn Baths in East Mesa
that he decided to bring the team west instead of returning to Miami, where the team trained in 1946. At least,
that's the line from former Buckhorn Baths owner Alice
Sliger.

It makes for a great story, and there's some truth to it. But
Horace Stoneham also made money as a real-estate
developer, and he wasn't shy about using his baseball
teams in association with his investments. In Arizona,
Stoneham ended up developing a resort in Casa Grande
after looking at other investments in the area. (He wasn't
the only developer to use a team as a lure; the New York
Yankees trained in Arizona to further the development
efforts of team owner Del Webb, who created the original

Sun City in the Phoenix area.) Stoneham also did the same thing in Minnesota as owner of the Minneapolis Millers, buying large parcels of suburban land for a potential ballpark site when he was looking to move the Giants there.

Still, there was certainly a real allure to the Buckhorm Baths, and a mineral bath there was a tradition for players training in the area. Leo Durocher was a devotee, as were Ernie Banks and Willie Mays. The mineral baths may not have been the major reason why Stoneham scheduled spring training in Phoenix, but it ended up being a major reason why the team returned—although, in fact, the team trained in Florida in 1951.

The Cactus League was born in 1954 when the Baltimore Orioles signed to train in Yuma, joining the Indians, Cubs, and Giants in the state. Teams would come and go—the Red Sox replaced the Orioles in 1959, for instance—but more and more teams were attracted to Arizona after Veeck and Stoneham's arrival.

The Giants were replaced by the New York Yankees in 1951, under a unique one-year switch for the two franchises. Yankees co-owner Del Webb had extensive business dealings in Arizona, both as a developer (Pueblo Gardens in Tucson) and as a contractor (Hughes Missile Plant in Tucson), and he was eying other development opportunities in the state. (He would later launch Sun City, the groundbreaking senior community in the Phoenix suburbs.) What better way to promote the Del Webb Corporation than a Yankees spring tenure in Phoenix?

The expansion Angels played some games in Arizona in 1961 despite training in Palm Springs, California, while the expansion Houston Colt .45s played at Geronimo Park in Apache Junction. Most were lured with economic incentives: communities were all too willing to build facilities for teams, who benefited from a

growing fan base (i.e.: transplanted retirees) and a growing economy. Some decisions, however, were more accidental. When the
Seattle Pilots moved to Milwaukee in 1970, owner Bud Selig
decided to keep the team's training base in Arizona, since he win-
tered in Scottsdale.

After the Cubs and Red Sox departed in 1966, the Cactus League
was down to a troubling four teams, with two of those—the
Angels and Cubs—training in California. (Over the years, teams
continued to shift between Arizona and Florida: the Indians,
Rangers, Royals, Red Sox, and Orioles have trained in both
states.)

Changes in the 1969 spring training season saved the league. The
Oakland Athletics moved to Mesa's Rendezvous Park (later
Hohokam Stadium; the team returned there in 2015) after team
owner Charlie O. Finley flirted with cities like Chandler in previous years, the expansion San Diego Padres began training at
Yuma's Desert Sun Stadium, and the Seattle Pilots set up spring
operations in Tempe Diablo Stadium.

By 1977, there were eight teams training in Arizona.

Baseball's move toward the West also hastened the growth of the
Cactus League: with the Los Angeles Dodgers' relocation to a
Glendale training facility, all eight Western MLB teams now train
in Arizona. If you're running the Seattle Mariners or the San
Diego Padres, an Arizona locale makes it far easier for fans and
the media to attend spring training.

Today, the Cactus League is a lively institution in Phoenix. The
2010 arrival of the Cincinnati Reds gave Arizona 15 teams, the
most in the Cactus League's history. We've seen new and renovated facilities emerge the last several years, as demand for baseball still continues to grow. For baseball fans, it's an abundance of
riches, as you're never too far from a practice or a game no matter
where you are in the Valley of the Sun.

Photo: Scottsdale Charros in the 1950s. The Charros still run spring training at Scottsdale Stadium.

TOURING PHOENIX AND SCOTTSDALE

With 15 teams training in the region, the Valley of the Sun hosts the entire Cactus League, combining the spirit of the Wild West with a bustling economy and a diverse population to create one of the largest metropolitan areas in the country.

Understanding diversity (and we don't mean that in a politically correct way) is the key to understanding the greater Phoenix area. Spend any time in the area and you realize that there's no "one" Phoenix; instead, Phoenix is made up of interconnected communities, and part of the fun is exploring the many facets of the Phoenix area. And while we refer to Phoenix, we're really referring to the general area: only one team, the Milwaukee Brewers, trains in Phoenix proper.

Greater Phoenix is made up of the following areas:

- Downtown Phoenix used to be a ghost town after hours, but it's now the city's sports and entertainment center. Normally Chase Field, the home of the Arizona Diamondbacks, is empty until the end of spring training, when the Diamondbacks usually schedule a few exhibition games to put the ballpark through its paces. In addition, baseball fans tend to hang around downtown sports bars like Cooper'stown (which we'll discuss later).
- The Camelback Corridor is a repository of serious money in the Valley. Many corporations call this area home, while much of the high-end shopping in the region can be found there as well.
- Scottsdale is the upscale part of town, but downtown Scottsdale is also home to an area celebrating the Wild West and Phoenix's place in the settling of the West. (We'll discuss Scottsdale in more detail in the San Francisco Giants chapter.)
- Tempe is home to Arizona State University, considered one of the best party colleges in the country. The action—both with bars and restaurants—takes place along or near Mill Avenue in Tempe. (We'll discuss Tempe in more depth in the Los Angeles Angels of Anaheim and Chicago Cubs chapters.)
- Mesa is largely a residential area to the east of Tempe. (We'll discuss Mesa in more depth in the Oakland Athletics chapter.)
- The northwestern and western suburbs have evolved into their own little spring-training worlds, with six teams training in four facilities. At times Surprise, Goodyear, Glendale, and Peoria really don't feel like part of the Valley of the Sun, as they're made up mainly of newer developments.

Navigating the Valley of the Sun

Despite its size, the Valley of the Sun is surprisingly easy to navigate. Once you master your location relative to the freeways or to one of the major streets in the region, you stand a much better chance of not getting lost in a new area.

Why? Because the entire region is built in a grid system extending to the outer regions of the area. Freeways and bypasses intersect the grid at convenient points, making Phoenix easy and convenient to navigate.

Two major freeways service the area: I-10 and I-17. I-10 enters the region from the west, where it's known as the Papago Freeway, running through the center of Phoenix and then heading south to Tempe and Tucson. This is the one freeway you'll spend some time driving, as it's the best way to reach the western and northwestern suburbs. I-17 (Black Canyon Freeway) comes in from the north and loops south of downtown before merging with I-10 (the merged stretch is called the Maricopa Freeway) near Sky Harbor International Airport.

Highway 60 (Grand Avenue) runs through the northwest quadrant of the region from downtown Phoenix all the way past Surprise. When you look at maps, you'll be tempted to take Highway 60 from the center of town to Peoria and Surprise. Don't. Highway 60 is filled with stop lights and traffic and is rarely worth the fuss. Instead, use Highway 101 as a shortcut. Highway 101 loops around the north side of town and is a true freeway. To go to Peoria from downtown, the quickest way is not the most direct way—Highway 60—but rather taking Highway 10 to Highway 101 and then heading north. Highway 101 is also the fastest way to reach the Maryvale neighborhood, Peoria, and Surprise.

INSIDER'S TIP
You won't see Maryvale on the map. Technically, Maryvale

is a Phoenix neighborhood, located in the southwestern part of Phoenix. With the move of the Oakland Athletics from Phoenix Municipal Stadium to Mesa's Hohokam Stadium, the Milwaukee Brewers are the only team to train within Phoenix city limits. Every other team trains in the suburbs.

Once in the city, there are some major streets that will get you anywhere: Washington Street, Buckeye Road, Van Buren Street, McDowell Road, Thomas Road, Indian School Road, and Camelback Road are all major east-west streets that will usually get you close to where you want to go.

INSIDER'S TIP

You can easily figure out the approximate location of an address. All addresses begin at Central Avenue (which runs north-south through downtown) and Washington Street (which runs east-west through downtown). Streets are on the east side of town, while avenues are on the west side of town. Camelback Street is 50 blocks north of Washington Street, so you can usually determine where you are relative to Camelback and Washington.

Arriving in Phoenix

Sky Harbor International Airport is the major airport in the region. It is also one of the most confusing airports in the United States, thanks to a poor design that splits the airport into three terminals. If you're planning on meeting friends in the Phoenix airport, don't plan on merely meeting by the luggage claim. There are three separate terminals, and so there are three separate luggage claims.

And you will want to rent a car unless you plan on spending all your time directly next to a ballpark. We'll say it again: Phoenix sprawls, and no one walks. Public transit is good if you want to get around the center city but is completely lacking for those making their way to spring-training facilities. To make your way around in

Phoenix, a car is essential; parking is almost always free and plentiful.

Sky Harbor International Airport, 3400 E. Sky Harbor Blvd., Phoenix; 602/273-3300; phxskyharbor.com.

INSIDER'S TIP
Even though the Valley sprawls, the spring-training sites are conveniently located in relationship to the airport. To reach Scottsdale from the airport, take Hwy. 202 (the Red Mountain Freeway) to Hwy. 101. To reach downtown Phoenix, take I-10 west. To reach Surprise or Peoria, take I-10 west to Hwy. 101 north. To reach Glendale or Goodyear, take I-10 west. To reach Tempe or Mesa, take I-10 or Hwy. 60 (the Superstition Freeway).

A smaller airport, Phoenix-Mesa Gateway, features flights from Allegiant Airlines, which serves many midsized and smaller markets nationally—the likes of Bozeman, Rockford, Bellingham, Cincinnati, Oakland, and Stockton. Alamo, Enterprise, and Hertz have facilities there. *Phoenix-Mesa Gateway Airport, 6033 S. Sossaman Rd., Mesa; phxmesagateway.org.*

Phoenix Attractions

With so many spring-training facilities in a concentrated area, you'll be able to hit at least one game daily during your stay, or two if the scheduling gods are smiling upon you and someone has arranged a night game. (This is now easier than it once was. While MLB teams don't schedule many night games, Arizona State University plays most of its home slate at Phoenix Municipal Stadium in the evening.) You'll spend much of your time at the ballpark, but you will probably want a few more diversions during the course of your stay. There's something for everyone in Phoenix; we'll list some of the more popular indoor and outdoor attractions here. (The many attractions of Scottsdale are listed later in this chapter.) Here we'll pass along some family-friendly activities.

Camelback Mountain, located in the northeast part of town, is a popular destination for hikers and nature lovers. There are four trails—two for inexperienced hikers, running less than an eighth of a mile, and two for very experienced hikers, reaching 1.5 miles. You can find parking for the various trails at East McDonald Drive and Tatum Boulevard. Some warning: even on the shorter trails you run some risk of dehydration and sunburn, so bring water and sunscreen.

The Desert Botanical Garden is 50 acres of trails and exhibits covering the ecosystem of the Sonoran desert. It's home to 139 endangered species of plants, as well as the most cacti you've seen in your life. *Desert Botanical Garden, 1201 N. Galvin Pkwy., Phoenix; 480/941-1225; dbg.org. Adults, $22; seniors, $20; children (13-18), $12; children (3-12), $10.*

Another great hiking spot: Papago Park. For those just wanting to get outside, there are some nice level trails through the desert brush, perfect for those of us who might not be in perfect shape after a long winter. (Remember: stay hydrated.) For those wanting a challenge, check out the rock-climbing trails. *Papago Park, 625 N. Galvin Pkwy., Phoenix; 602/495-5458; phoenix.gov/parks/ trails/locations/papago/index.html.*

Located near both the Desert Botanical Garden and Papago Park is the Phoenix Zoo, a great place to take the kids. The layout is organized by theme—there are separate trails with African, Tropical, and Arizona themes, along with a Children's Trail. There are over 1,300 animals on display, and traversing the whole place should take about three hours. *Phoenix Zoo, 455 N. Galvin Pkwy., Phoenix; 602/273-1341; phoenixzoo.org. Adults, $20; seniors, $17; children 3-12, $12.*

Architecture buffs will be fascinated by Taliesin West, Frank

Lloyd Wright's winter home, and the Biltmore, inspired by Wright's architecture style. Located in Scottsdale, Taliesin West takes its inspiration from the Arizona landscape; like all Wright buildings, the scale is intimate and low to the ground, while almost all of the materials were locally sourced. *Taliesin West, 12621 Frank Lloyd Wright Blvd., Scottsdale; 480/860-2700; franklloyd-wright.org. Prices range depending on length of tour.*

The Arizona Biltmore may be the most unique hotel in Phoenix. Located in the Camelback Corridor, the Arizona Biltmore was designed by Albert Chase McArthur, a former student of Frank Lloyd Wright, who served as the consulting architect. The Wright influence is obvious: the hotel is constructed of precast concrete blocks (a building material favored by Wright) in a unique geometric pattern. The blocks were designed by local artist Emry Kopta in a unique "Biltmore Block" pattern. Chewing-gum magnate William Wrigley, Jr. was an early investor in the project, and by 1930 owned the entire place, but curiously he never combined it with his other great passion, the Chicago Cubs, who instead trained for many of the Wrigley years on California's Catalina Island. During the 1930s and 1940s, it was the place to winter in Phoenix; Irving Berlin wrote "White Christmas" while lounging poolside at the Biltmore. Stop by The Wright Bar even if you're not staying there; the lobby is an oasis and a nice place for a post-game cocktail. *Arizona Biltmore, 2400 E. Missouri Av., Phoenix; 800/950-0086; arizonabiltmore.com.*

Speaking on the Camelback Corridor: a pleasant evening can be spent at the Biltmore Fashion Park. All the major trendy stores are represented in the open-air mall, but our preference is to do dinner at True Food Kitchen or Seasons 52, poke around at the Apple Store, and then stop for a treat at the Paradise Bakery. *Biltmore Fashion Park, 24th St. and Camelback Rd., Phoenix; 602/955-8400; shopbiltmore.com.*

The Heard Museum focuses on indigenous peoples of the Americas, with an emphasis on American Indian tribes and other cultures of the Southwest. It's that Southwestern focus you'll want to explore. *The Heard Museum, 2301 N. Central Av., Phoenix; 602/252-8840; heard.org.* Adults, $18; seniors $13.50, children, $7.50.

These is much more to the greater Phoenix area than just these highlights. We go into depth on the areas surrounding the ballparks in the following chapters.

Recommended Phoenix Restaurants

There is an amazing diversity of restaurants in the Valley of the Sun. The region helped make Southwestern cuisine one of the most innovative food movements of the last 20 years, and today you can find world-class restaurants throughout the region. You can also find a wide range of sports bars and restaurants, too, if your tastes don't run to haute cuisine. In this section, we'll give you a little of each. We also will list recommended restaurants close to each of the spring-training ballparks.

Cooper'stown is a mandatory stop during Cactus League spring training, even if no team is near Chase Field, the regular-season home of the Arizona Diamondbacks. Cooper'stown, located two blocks from Chase Field, was created by baseball fanatic and rocker Alice Cooper, who settled in Phoenix after his shock-rock days and was looking for a new challenge. The result is an entertainment complex featuring a restaurant and outdoor stage with frequent live music. Think of a Hard Rock Cafe run by sports geeks, and you have a pretty good vision of the sports and rock memorabilia dominating the interior. And yes, Alice Cooper does spend quite a bit of time hanging around.

The fare is fairly eclectic for a theme restaurant: there's the Ryne Sandburger, BBQ and more. Cooper'stown does its own smoking on the premises, so the ribs are recommended. Fans of home cooking will appreciate the tuna-noodle casserole made from Mama

Cooper's recipe. If you're famished, consider The Big Unit, a $25, two-foot-long hot dog named after the Diamondbacks' Randy Johnson (an original investor in the restaurant). But be prepared for a fuss if you do: sirens go off when a customer orders one. *Alice Cooper'stown, 101 E. Jackson St., Phoenix; 602/253-7337; alicecooperstown.com.*

In the same vein (sans the rock and roll) is Majerle's Sports Grill, also located in downtown Phoenix. Dan Majerle ("Mar-ley") was a popular forward for the Phoenix Suns, and when US Airways Arena (now Talking Stick Resort Arena) was completed in 1992, the 3-point sharpshooter went into the sports-bar business and opened up Majerle's in the oldest commercial building in down-town Phoenix. *Majerle's Sports Grill, 24 N. 2nd St., Phoenix; 602/ 253-0118; majerles.com.*

If you find yourself in the vicinity of Chase Field at night after a few cocktails, drop by Lo-Lo's Chicken and Waffles. Phoenix isn't known for its soul food, but Lo-Lo's is in a class by itself when it comes to that magic combination of chicken and waf-fles—a much better pairing than you'd think. *Lo-Lo's Chicken and Waffles, 1220 S. Central Av., Phoenix; 602/340-1304; loloschicke-nandwaffles.com.* Also popular and newer: the Scottsdale location. *3133 N. Scottsdale Rd., Scottsdale; 480/945-1920.*

Considerably more upscale is the Barrio Cafe, which bills itself as modern Mexican. Reviewers near and far rave about the Barrio Cafe and are amazed that owner/chef Silvana Salcido Esparza decided to locate a haute cuisine establishment in a transitional neighborhood. The menu changes monthly, but there are some items always available. Be sure to have the Guacamole Casero, prepared tableside: it's a ripe avocado moistened with olive oil and mashed with onions, cilantro, tomato, and pomegranate seeds. As for the rest of the menu: mole fans will want to check out the *enchiladas de mole*, while the *cochinita pibil* (slow roasted pork with *achiote rojo*) is excellent. Wash it down with a horchata, a sweet Mexican drink made of rice, cinnamon, lime juice, and water.

It is a little unfair to deem the offerings at the Barrio Cafe haute cuisine: excellent food served at a reasonable price in a neighborhood cafe. The place is small (seating only 69) and fills up quickly; if you're not there right at opening time (5:30 p.m.), be prepared for a wait, even if you do make a reservation. Highly recommended. *Barrio Cafe, 2814 N. 16th St., Phoenix; 602/636-0240; barriocafe.com.*

For Mexican seafood, check out Mariscos Playa Hermosa. We think of Mexican cuisine as being a monolithic entity, but regional flavors are important south of the border. In the case of Mariscos Playa Hermosa, the cuisine is not only Mexican but specializes in the seafood cuisine found in Hermosillo. You normally don't think of great seafood when you think of landlocked Phoenix, but Mariscos Playa Hermosa shatters that stereotype. *Mariscos Playa Hermosa, 1605 E. Garfield St., Phoenix; 602/462-1563; mariscos-playahermosa.com.*

Phoenix has more than its share of steakhouses, and one of the more notable ones is Rustlers Rooste. Whether you buy into the mythology of the place—that the restaurant was formerly a hideaway for cattle rustlers—there's no doubt that the Rooste provides an impressive view of the Valley. Most will order steak; the adventurous will order rattlesnake. *Rustler's Rooste, 8383 S. 48th St., Phoenix; 602/431-6474; rustlersrooste.com.*

This doesn't even scrape the surface of good restaurants in Phoenix; we're not even going near the likes of Tarbell's or Tomaso's, both located in the Camelback Corridor. These are some opening suggestions, but you don't ever have to go very far throughout the entire region to find some good food.

INSIDER'S TIP
Remember that all the spring-training facilities in Phoenix

are fairly close together. It's easy to move around the city, so don't assume that just because an attraction or restaurant is in Scottsdale or Tempe you should avoid it. Tempe, Scottsdale, Mesa, and Phoenix are all adjoining communities, as are Peoria and Surprise. We list hotels and restaurants by locale, but don't let these boundaries stop you from perusing the chapters for all the ballparks in search of a restaurant or attraction: you're never really far away from anything in the Valley of the Sun.

Scottsdale: Upscale Meets Kitsch

Downtown Scottsdale is a curious mix of the kitsch and the artsy; it's where the well-heeled in the region step out to buy a cowboy T-shirt for the grandkids and then dine at an upscale restaurant before hitting the well-regarded Scottsdale Art Museum.

Of course, another way to put it is that Scottsdale has something for everyone, ranging from a slew of touristy Old West shops in Old Town to the upscale department stores at the Scottsdale Fashion Mall. This all means you can easily entertain yourself for days in Scottsdale between spring-training games in the Valley.

There are four major districts to downtown Scottsdale: Fifth Avenue, Main Street, Old Town, and Marshall Way. Fifth Avenue features upscale shopping and dining; the Marshall Way Arts District features art galleries specializing in contemporary art from local artists, as well as a wide variety of regionally produced jewelry; Main Street is one of the largest concentrations of art galleries in the world; and Old Town features the aforementioned Wild West kitsch.

The San Francisco Giants play at Scottsdale Stadium, which we'll cover in its own chapter.

Spring-Training Traditions: Don and Charlie's & The Pink Pony

Scottsdale is home to two restaurants that strongly embody the spring-training traditions in the area. For many, a visit to one or both restaurants is a must.

Don & Charlie's dates back only to 1981, but it has become a spring-training tradition. Yes, the menu is geared toward the masculine—ribs and steaks are the highlights—and Don Carson is a lifelong baseball fan who has covered the walls with sports memorabilia. He's also one of the most connected guys in the sports world for someone not actually working for a sports team. There aren't many of those old-time restaurateurs left in the world; in the old days, every city had a low-key place catering to athletes and fans, but they've been replaced by loud sports bars featuring a gazillion flat screens.

You'll see Don working the room most nights during spring training; with a little prompting, he may even sit down and share a few memories of spring training with you. It's an unusual night when some sort of MLB type isn't in attendance: our last three or so visits have always featured the sight of Bob Uecker holding court. Don and Charlie's tends to be pretty packed in spring training; a reservation is recommended, especially on the weekend.

> **INSIDER'S TIP**
> You can reserve a table at Don & Charlie's via the Open Table website. We'd recommend doing so; waits during spring training are measured by the hour, not the minute.

> **INSIDER'S TIP**
> If you are on Facebook, check out the restaurant's page. Don updates it himself, ruminating on sporting events, dinner specials, and whether or not ranch dressing should be an option. (Answer: apparently yes.)

As a bonus: the food at Don & Charlie's is pretty good, with any form of meat—steaks, ribs, burger bar—worth ordering. *Don & Charlie's, 7501 E. Camelback Rd., Scottsdale; 480/990-0900; donandcharlies.com.*

The Pink Pony has been renovated under new ownership after a few closures. Gone is the old-timey look left unchanged since it opened in 1952; what's there is a mix of modern mid-century décor—fitting perfectly within Scottsdale—along with baseball memorabilia. You'll walk across the original Scottsdale Stadium home plate upon entering the restaurant. Gone are the Naugahyde booths and Gene Autry's favorite table, but the emphasis here is still on spring training. (The photo at the beginning of this chapter shows the old Pink Pony, via Experience Scottsdale.) *The Pink Pony, 3831 N. Scottsdale Rd., Scottsdale; 480/945-6697; pinkponyscottsdale.com.*

Other Scottsdale Baseball Hotspots

Scottsdale has traditionally been the center of spring training in the Valley of the Sun. While that's not necessarily true anymore, it's certainly home to the most restaurants catering to spring-training fans and baseball nostalgia. Besides the two restaurants featured in the previous section, there are other dining and drinking establishments that have been attracting spring-training fans for decades.

Bob and Mary Brower catered to baseball fans and players at the Coach House in Scottsdale; of course, this was back in the 1960s and the Boston Red Sox was the team training in Scottsdale. But some things remain the same: The Brower family still owns the Coach House, and it's still a spring-training hangout. It's not uncommon to see a player or three relaxing with an adult beverage on the patio of Scottsdale's oldest tavern. *Coach House, 7011 E. Indian School Rd., Scottsdale; 480/990-3433; coachhousescottsdale.com.*

Another restaurant in Old Town Scottsdale with ties to spring training is The Italian Grotto. A traditional player haunt, The Grotto is a sports bar cum traditional Italian restaurant, with lots of pasta on the menus and lots of sports memorabilia on the walls. *3915 North Scottsdale Rd., Scottsdale; 480/994-1489; italian-grotto.restaurantengine.com.*

More a hangout for sportswriters than for players or coaches (yes, there are still writers with boots on the ground in spring training, as opposed to bloggers opining from their desk next to the basement water heater), Karsen's Grill is another traditional Old Town spring-training hangout. *Karsen's Grill, 7246 East 1st St. #101, Scottsdale; 480/990-7660.*

Scottsdale Dining and Drinking

Apart from the traditional choices, downtown Scottsdale features a wide range of dining and drinking options in all sorts of genres and price ranges. Though this is a fairly extensive list of restaurants and hotspots, it's by no means a complete list.

Our favorite spot before a Giants home game at Scottsdale Stadium is the Sugar Bowl Ice Cream Parlor. The specialty, as you might expect, is ice cream (try the top hat sundae), but the menu also features tasty sandwiches and burgers. It's the most kid-friendly place in downtown Scottsdale—and that extends to Giants minor-leaguers as well, as they'll occasionally show up for a treat after practice. And yes, plenty of adults hit the place for some comfort without kids in tow. Expect to wait for a table at lunch or dinner. *Sugar Bowl Ice Cream Parlor, 4005 N. Scottsdale Rd., Scottsdale; 480/946-0051; sugarbowlscottsdale.com.*

Though there are several Zipps sports bars in Phoenix, our favorite is Zipps Sports Grill Camelback, in the middle of Old Town Scottsdale. It's a great place to follow March Madness; the outdoor deck features TVs and a firepit, perfect for viewing those evening basketball games. *Zipps Sports Grill Camelback, 7551 E. Camelback Rd., Scottsdale; 480/970-9507; zippssportsgrills.com.*

Citizen Public House is an upscale gastropub a longish walk from Scottsdale Stadium. It's more on the upscale side of the equation, with an above-average drink lineup and an eclectic food lineup that includes a great buttermilk fried chicken, the inevitable flat-iron steak, and more. Management has worked hard to attract Giants fans, and the effort has paid off. *Citizen Public House, 7111 E. 5th Av., Scottsdale; 480/398-4208; citizenpublic-house.com.*

Another upscale restaurant in Old Town worth a visit: FnB, an upscale gastropub with an emphasis on farm-to-table cuisine, complete with an Arizona-only wine program. *FnB, 7125 E. 5th Av., #31, Scottsdale; 480-284-4777; fnbrestaurant.com.*

Four Peaks is the top microbrewery in the Valley of the Sun, and the firm has branched out past its very popular Tempe location with a Scottsdale outpost. A full range of Four Peaks brews are on tap (our fave on a hot March day: the Hefeweizen), while a full menu of burgers, pizzas, and appetizers is available until 1 a.m. (We discuss Four Peaks Tempe in our Tempe Diablo Stadium chapter.) *Four Peaks Grill & Tap, 15745 N. Hayden Rd., Scotts-dale; 480/991-1795; fourpeaks.com.*

Two Brothers Scottsdale Taphouse is an absolutely zoo on a week-end night, and with good reason: the attractively designed restau-rant/brewhouse has a wide variety of tasty beers, especially unique offerings from the brewery's 10-barrel brewing system. Five of these unique locally brewed beers are always on tap. *Two Brothers Scottsdale Taphouse, 4321 N. Scottsdale Av., Scottsdale; 480-378-3001; twobrothersbrewing.com.*

Live music and cheap beer are featured at Old Town Tavern, where bands are scheduled every day the Giants are playing at Scottsdale Stadium. It's a small space and within a short walk of

Scottsdale Stadium, so get there early for a table and cheap ($3)
Sierra Nevada Pale Ale or Anchor Steam. *7320 E. Scottsdale Rd.
Scottsdale; 480/945-2882; oldtowntavernaz.com.*

The Blue Moose is another downtown sports bar of note within a
short walk of Scottsdale Stadium. The half-pound burger will keep
you filled for a day or two. Be sure to sit out on the expanded deck
before the game. *Blue Moose, 7373 E. Scottsdale Mall, Scottsdale;
480/949-7959; thebluemoosescottsdale.com.*

If you like your Italian cuisine without a Mediterranean influence,
Cowboy Ciao features modern Italian cuisine with a Tex-Mex
twist. *7133 E. Stetson Dr., Scottsdale; 480/946-3111; cowboy-
ciao.com.*

More casual dining can be found at Flicka's Baja Cantina, especially on the 3,000-square-foot patio overlooking Scottsdale Road.
Yes, it is a little odd to design a deck with a nautical look in the
middle of the desert, but the approach works, especially when
complimented by a menu that includes fish tacos and cheap PBRs.
*Flicka's Bar & Grill, 2003 N. Scottsdale Rd., Scottsdale; 480/
945-3618; flickasbajacantina.com.*

Old Town Tortilla Factory is located in a 75-year-old adobe home
in the heart of Old Town Scottsdale and features a 1,200-square-
foot deck. The margaritas served here have won national acclaim,
and it's hard to imagine anything better than sipping an excellent
margarita under a clear desert sky at night. *Old Town Tortilla Factory, 6910 E. Main St.; 480/945-4567; oldtowntortillafactory.com.*

Dos Gringos features good food, a huge patio, and cheap beer. *Dos
Gringos, 4209 N. Craftsman Court, Scottsdale; 480/423-3800;
dosgringosaz.com.*

And then there's the Salty Senorita, which is basically Hooters
with a Mexican twist. Perhaps that's not quite fair; the place also
specializes in a wide selection of tequilas. But the atmosphere is

definitely a party one, and the deck is definitely a hopping place after a Giants game. If you're interested, Scottsdale Stadium features Salty Senorita margaritas in the concessions stands. *Salty Senorita, 3636 N. Scottsdale Rd., Scottsdale; 480/946-SALTY; saltysenorita.com.*

Order yourself a man drink (scotches and bourbons dominate the drink menu) at AZ 88 and hang out with the sleek and sexy of Scottsdale on the gorgeous patio. North of the Scottsdale Museum of Contemporary Art, AZ 88 is the embodiment of Scottsdale chic. *AZ 88, 7353 Scottsdale Mall, Scottsdale; 480/994-5576; az88.com.*

Patsy Grimaldi's Coal Brick-Oven Pizzeria is definitely an oddity or a pleasant surprise, depending on your point of view. We're not exactly sure how one of the best pizzerias in Brooklyn ended up with a Scottsdale outpost, but we're too busy scarfing down the thin-crust pizza to care. For those who don't worship the perfect pizza, there are calzones on the menu as well. *Patsy Grimaldi's Coal Brick-Oven Pizzeria, 4000 N. Scottsdale Rd., Scottsdale; 480/994-1100; grimaldispizzeria.com.*

Old Town Scottsdale

Scottsdale is not a very old community: it began life as a housing development in 1894 when an Eastern banker named Albert Utley divided 40 acres of desert land into lots. The name Scottsdale comes from U.S. Chaplain Winfield Scott, whose promotional efforts attracted many of the earlier settlers.

Most of today's Old Town in downtown Scottsdale dates back to the 1920s or earlier, when the area experienced its first growth spurt. There are several remnants of the original Scottsdale in the Old Town area:

- Cavalliere Blacksmith (*3805 N. Brown Av.; 480/ 945-6262*). George Cavalliere moved his family to

Scottsdale in 1910 and opened a blacksmith shop on the edge of downtown Scottsdale. He originally set up shop in a metal building, which he replaced with the current adobe structure in 1920. The Cavalliere family still operates the blacksmith shop.

- The first post office in Scottsdale opened in 1928 and was a community gathering place when the mail was delivered from Phoenix. The building still stands and is now home to Porter's Western Wear (*3944 N. Brown Av.; 480/945-0868*).
- Our Lady of Perpetual Help Catholic Church (*3817 N. Brown Av.*) is a striking white building in Old Town. It dates back to 1933 when local Mexican residents volunteered their time and money to construct the church.
- The Little Red Schoolhouse (*7333 Scottsdale Mall; 480/945-4499*), now home to a local historical society, was built in 1909 as a two-room schoolhouse. It housed the school through the 1960s and was then used for a variety of civic purposes.
- Los Olivos Restaurant (*7328 E. 2nd St.; 946/225-6480*), built in the 1950s, originally housed a pool hall and a church before becoming a Mexican restaurant.
- The Rusty Spur Saloon (*7245 E. Main St.; 480/941-2628; rustyspursaloon.com*) originally was the Farmer's State Bank of Scottsdale when the building opened in 1921. The bank didn't last long, closing during the Great Depression. Today it's one of Scottsdale's oldest bars, opening as a bar in 1951.

There's one other feature in Old Town worth checking out: the olive trees along Drinkwater Boulevard and Second Street. Winfield Scott, the founder of Scottsdale, planted them in 1896.

Other Sports in the Area

In the unlikely event you have a spare moment during your spring trip to Phoenix, there are plenty of other sporting events to occupy your time.

Phoenix is a major-league city, and both NBA and NHL games are scheduled in March. The Phoenix Suns play at the downtown Talking Stick Resort Arena, one of the more intimate facilities in the NBA. Buy your tickets early; the Suns are a major draw. *Talking Stick Resort Arena, 201 E. Jefferson St., Phoenix; 602/ 379-7800; talkingstickresortarena.com.*

If major-league hockey is more to your liking, the NHL's Arizona Coyotes play at Gila River Arena in Glendale, near the Dodgers/ White Sox, Mariners/Padres, Brewers and Reds/Indians camps. Arizona Coyotes? Gila River Arena? Yes, things have changed a little in Glendale, where new Coyotes owners are working hard to bring back interest in hockey in a renovated arena. It always feels a little weird to us to be sipping cocktails in 80-degree weather and then heading into a hermetically sealed area to see ice hockey, but apparently there are enough expatriate Canadians and Minnesotans in the Phoenix area to support an NHL team—at least for now. *Gila River Arena, 9400 W. Maryland Av., Glendale; 623/ 772-3200; gilariverarena.com.*

A free evening could entail a visit to see the Arizona State University Sun Devils playing at Phoenix Municipal Stadium, the former spring home of the Oakland Athletics. The Sun Devils formerly played on campus at Winkles Field-Packard Stadium at Brock Ballpark (known by most locals as Packard Stadium), but the decision was made to tear down the ballpark to make way for development, which in turn is funding improvements to Sun Devil Stadium. The ASU baseball program is traditionally strong, so we'll be covering the Sun Devils and Phoenix Muni in their own chapter.

Phoenix/Scottsdale and the Wild West

The mythology of the Wild West is still strong in Arizona: the state is an essentially conservative place where citizens take great pride in the frontier spirit exemplified in the Wild West ethos.

Where mythology ends and caricature begins is another issue, of course—not every pioneer was as funny as Gabby Hayes, as heroic as Tom Mix, as black-hearted as Wyatt Earp, or tuneful as Gene Autry—but there's just enough truth to the tales of the Wild West to reverberate in today's culture.

There are many outposts in Phoenix celebrating one vision or another of the Wild West. If you're bringing your kids to spring training, chances are pretty good they'd enjoy some exposure to the Wild West.

One of the bigger Wild West attractions in Scottsdale is the Rawhide Steakhouse and Saloon, a recreation of an 1880s Arizona town. This Wild West adventure includes train and stagecoach rides, outdoor cookouts, gunfights, and gold panning. Grownups will appreciate the cowboy steaks and cold beer. *Rawhide Steakhouse & Saloon, 5700 W. North Loop Rd., Chandler; 480/502-6500; rawhide.com.*

Beer in the Valley

The natural accompaniment to baseball and spring training? Good beer. And it's a good day when you can combine outstanding beer with a sunny day at the ballpark. Whether it's a notable brew at the ballpark, a pregame brew at a watering spot near training camp, or a brewpub for a postgame dinner, you'll have plenty of great choices during your Cactus League trip.

We cover lots of brewpubs and breweries in the chapters covering specific training camps: proximity counts, of course. Here are some additional recommendations for worthy brewpubs and brew-eries. Some are in the suburbs far from spring-training camps, but unless you plan on spending eight hours a day in camp, you'll have time to drive to Chandler or Gilbert to hit one of these notable beer spots. In any case, the Valley of the Sun has trans-formed in the last five or so years from a beer desert to a brewery oasis. Here are our choices for brewpubs and breweries worth the drive, in addition to the breweries and brewpubs listed elsewhere in this chapter.

We discuss Four Peaks plenty of times in the course of this book, but it's not an understatement to say the company has been a leader in the expansion of brewing in the Valley. The psychic cen-ter for this growth is the firm's original brewpub in Tempe, an easy drive from Sloan Park, Scottsdale Stadium, and Hohokam Stadium. There are plenty of worthy alternatives to Four Peaks, however. Here is a list of our favorite watering holes, listed by city. The common denominator: these are all venues that are defi-nitely worth a drive.

- SanTan Brewing Co. (8 S. San Marcos Place, Chandler; 480/917-8700; santanbrewing.com).
- Arizona Wilderness Brewing Co (721 N. Arizona Av., Gilbert; 480/284-9863; azwbeer.com)
- Attic Ale House (4247 E. Indian School Rd., Phoenix; 602/955-1967; theatticaz.com)
- Mother Bunch Brewery (825 N. 7th St, Phoenix; 602/368-3580; motherbunchbrew.com)
- OHSO Brewery (4900 E. Indian School Rd., Phoenix; 602/955-0358; ohsobrewery.com)
- Phoenix Ale Brewery (3002 E. Washington St., Phoenix; 602/275-5049; phoenixale.com)
- Sonoran Brewing Co. (3002 E. Washington St., Phoenix; 602/510-8996; sonoranbrewing.com)
- SunUp Brewing Co. (322 E. Camelback Rd., Phoenix; 602/279-8909; sunup.beer)

- Wren House Brewing Co. (2125 N. 24th St., Phoenix; 602/244-9184; wrenhousebrewing.com)
- Papago Brewing (Papago Plaza Shopping Center, 7107 E. McDowell Rd., Scottsdale; 480/425-7439; papagobrewing.com)
- Scottsdale Beer Co. (8608 E. Shea Blvd., Scottsdale; 480/219-1844; scottsdalebeercompany.com)
- Huss Brewing Co. (1520 W. Mineral Rd., Tempe; 480/264-7611; hussbrewing.com)
- Sleepy Dog Brewery (1920 E. University Dr., #104, Tempe; 480/967-5476; sleepydogbrewing.com)

CAMELBACK RANCH-GLENDALE / CHICAGO WHITE SOX / LOS ANGELES DODGERS

QUICK FACTS

- **Capacity**: 13,000, plus standing room
- **Year Opened**: 2009
- **Dimensions**: 345L, 385LC, 410C, 385R, 345R
- **Dugout Locations**: Dodgers on the third-base side, White Sox on the first-base side
- **Practice Times**: Gates open at 9 a.m., with practices starting at 9:30 a.m.
- **Gates Open**: 90 minutes before game time, but gates to center-field courtyard, as well as concessions and team stores, open at 10:30 a.m. on game days. Home batting practice, until 11:15 a.m.; visitors batting practice, 11:15 a.m.-12:15 p.m.; visitors infield, 12:20-12:30 p.m.;

home infield, 12:30-12:40 p.m. Add six hours for a night
game.
- **Ticket Lines**: 800/905-3315
- **Address**: 10710 W. Camelback Rd., Phoenix, AZ 85037
- **Directions**: Take the Loop 101 (Agua Fria Loop) to the
Camelback Road exit. Turn west to the ballpark.

One with Nature in Glendale

One of the great joys of spring training is the informal nature of it
all. Fans look forward to getting up close and personal with players in a relaxed setting. Camelback Ranch–Glendale, spring home
of the Dodgers and White Sox, provides plenty of great memory-
making moments for fans old and young.

Camelback Ranch–Glendale is designed to appear to rise from the
flat Valley floor. A symmetrical two-building outpost in center
field houses the main ticket office, the largest team store and other
operations. The curved buildings immediately set the tone for the
spring experience at Camelback Ranch–Glendale.

The place is made for strolling. You are welcome to meander your way through the training complex before reaching the game, getting a chance to see multiple workouts on multiple diamonds. The experience is then topped with a game at one of the nicest ballparks in spring training.

But a spring-training complex must also fulfill all the needs of the main tenants. Both teams have state-of-the-art training facilities for both the major-league and minor-league squads, allowing both to smoothly run year-round operations. Fans don't see what happens behind the scenes—and most won't find things like weight rooms, aquatic treadmills, and multiple clubhouses very sexy or interesting, but both teams had the chance to spec out their operations spaces for their specific needs. The White Sox chose to put minor- and major-league facilities in the same building, though there are some differences in each section. The Dodgers, meanwhile, chose to break out the minor-league operations in a three-building complex, with separate buildings for training, support, and clubhouses. As with any modern training facility, there's video through the entire complex, giving coaches the chance to provide instant feedback to position players and pitchers.

The Glendale spring-training complex is one of the largest in the majors. The site, organized around a central connecting path and three-acre lake, hosts two ballpark entries—one at home plate and a more prominent entry at center field. Located on a 141-acre site, the ballpark has the capacity to host 13,500 fans. It includes more than 118,000 square feet of major- and minor-league clubhouses as well as four major-league practice fields, eight minor-league practice fields, and two practice infields. Each team has a replica major-league field to emulate their home ballpark.

Most fans will enter the ballpark at the parking lot located at West Camelback Road and 107th Avenue, west of the Camelback/I-101 interchange. This 1,000-plus parking lot is behind the grandstand. If the gates are open, you can cut across the ballpark to the practice fields past the center-field entrance; otherwise you'll need to walk around the perimeter to make your way to the practice field.

From the center-field entry, the White Sox training complex is on the right and the Dodgers' complex on the left. Each team has two MLB fields and four minor-league fields, as well as a half infield and specialized areas for sliding and bunting drills. A three-acre-plus pond, stocked with fish, separates the two training areas; besides serving as a holding pond for reclaimed water destined for watering the grounds, the pond serves an aesthetic function. Paths branch out from roughly the center of the complex to each team's MLB-sized practice fields.

The 141-acre site isn't purely symmetrical, reflecting each team's approach to player development. On the White Sox side, you have nothing but training fields; the main MLB field has limited access, with fans kept a distance from the players. On the Dodgers side, the main MLB practice field is almost totally open to fans. While there's seating (but no shade) in both practice fields, it's pretty clear the Dodgers want to encourage players to interact with fans—at least more than the White Sox brain trust does, for now. Heck, the Dodgers even installed a life-size Tommy Lasorda bob-blehead next to the practice field, and it's proven to be a big hit with fans.

As a fan, you're free to roam around most of it. The clubhouses are off limits—which is too bad, because they're gorgeous—and typically some of the practice fields are blocked off as well. Still, in terms of access, this is one of the most open spring complexes we've ever visited.

A symmetrical two-building outpost in center field houses the main ticket office, the large team store, and other operations. The curved buildings immediately set the tone for the spring experi-ence at Camelback Ranch–Glendale: the 14 buildings comprising the complex were designed to appear to rise from the flat Valley

floor, with sloping roofs, asymmetrical designs and organic
appearances. It also sits slightly off the trees in back of the batter's
eye, giving fans a view of the field and home plate as they
approach the field of play.

The ballpark seats 13,000 (10,500 fixed seats, the remainder on
the berm), but it feels smaller. Though the complex is set on 141
acres, the ballpark takes up a small part of that, and the combination of below-grade playing field and surrounding outbuildings
carves out an intimate space. The theme throughout the ballpark is
focused on natural materials and finishes; besides the gabion walls
so prominent in the outfield concourse, the buildings have a stone
or brown finish, and the outbuildings feature angled roofs
designed to feel like a natural part of the desert skyline. The seats
are done in a desert brown; surrounded by so many neutrals and
browns, the green grass is especially resplendent.

The suite/press box deck in back of home plate fits in with that
aesthetic as well. W-shaped supports give it a gentle rise over the
concourse, providing needed shade as well, though the existing
canopy really isn't large enough to shade much of the grandstand.
In an interesting twist, eight suites are mini-suites, seating only six
and sharing a buffet area. Spring training, teams are finding, is less
about the large corporate outings and more about smaller gather-
ings with friends and close business acquaintances. The move to
mini-suites, which is also happening on the MLB level to an
extent, makes sense for spring training.

As you sit in the grandstand, you'll see two buildings down each
line. Down the first-base line is the White Sox clubhouse/training
facility, and down the third-base line is the Dodgers major-league
clubhouse. Both teams will enter the field from the clubhouses,
albeit in slightly different ways: the White Sox will enter from a
truck entrance, while the Dodgers will enter through a small tunnel
under the outfield concourse and through the bullpen. You'll be

able to see each team from the concourse, but you won't be very close to the players.

When the game starts, take a good look at the second floor of the outfield buildings past the wraparound concourse, because that's where team officials will be. The Dodgers ownership commands a large suite and deck on the center-field side of the Los Angeles building while White Sox owner Jerry Reinsdorf has a smaller suite and deck on the center-field side of his building. The executive offices are spacious, but not sumptuous; both teams use the complexes as year-round training and development facilities, so the office space is needed.

In many ways the ballpark was designed to be low-impact. Gabion walls will probably confound visitors upon their first visit to the ballpark, but they fit in the design aesthetic. Gabion walls are retaining walls made of stacked stones enmeshed by wire; the wire keeps the rocks from scattering, and the weight of the stones makes for an efficient retaining wall. You'll find gabion walls throughout the outfield concourse at Camelback Ranch–Glendale. Also, the fields throughout the complex are watered with reclaimed water from a local wastewater facility.

Much of what makes the complex unique, sad to say, is out of view for most fans. The complex is designed to be a working facility, as the business of baseball now requires a 12-month approach to the game. Each team has separate, but basically equal training facilities, adapted for each team's needs. We're not going to get into the specifics of each facility here, but let's just say we cannot imagine a situation that wouldn't be addressed by one specialized space or another, whether it's the underwater treadmills in the hydrotherapy rooms, the spacious therapy rooms, the many media rooms, the plethora of meeting rooms, or the various video rooms. Both franchises field teams in the Arizona rookie league, and both send players to rehab under team supervision. And, of course, both teams are hoping players will settle in Phoenix in the winter and take advantage of the complex's workout facilities, batting cages, and more.

If you go, be prepared to make a day of it. You'll want to give yourself plenty of time to meander your way through the complex before the game, and it will take some time to make your way back to your car after the game. (Once there, it shouldn't take long to leave the ballpark; Camelback Road between the complex and the free was widened to four lanes and a center turn lane to accommodate spring-training crowds. There's still a bottleneck when you arrive, but exiting goes rather smoothly these days.) But go: Camelback Ranch–Glendale is one of the most scenic spring-training experiences in all of baseball.

The Spring-Training Ballpark Experience

Concessions

Lots of good meat-based products can be found at Camelback Ranch–Glendale: brats, Dodgers Dogs ($5.50; from Farmer John), Vienna Beef Chicago Dogs, Ditka sausages, smoked BBQ sandwiches, pastrami sandwiches, hamburgers, chili cheese fries, pizza, etc. A third-base-line stand offers a range of Mexican foods, with margaritas from local 3 Amigos Cantina. And the kids will like the shaved ice from a stand down the third-base line.

The beer selection runs the gamut between corporate brews and microbrews from the likes of Sam Adams and Pyramid.

The big thing about the food at Camelback Ranch–Glendale: it's not necessarily the quality (though a day with a Dodger Dog is a good day indeed), it's the accessibility. You're never too far from a concession stand.

INSIDER'S TIP
The Montejo Patio features a shaded area with plenty of food

and drink options, including bacon on a stick, pizza, kebobs, beer, and frozen margaritas.

Autographs

With so much accessibility to the training fields and two teams committed to accessibility, you will have plenty of opportunities to approach a player for a signature. Wandering the grounds before the game (get there at 10 a.m., when players are hitting the fields) will yield some autograph opportunities from players from both teams, even if their team is not scheduled to play that day. Before the game players from both teams will appear down the line and sign with no prompting from fans. After the game you'll find plenty of players approaching the stands for autographs as well.

Parking

One reason to come early to the ballpark: you can avoid the long lines of fans entering the parking lots. Camelback Road was widened to four lanes when the ballpark was under construction, but it wasn't enough. Crowds at Camelback Ranch–Glendale are notoriously late late to arrive—especially those Dodgers fans!—so arriving early is the best way to avoid the Camelback Road traffic.

The parking situation at Camelback Ranch–Glendale has changed over the years. Originally the main parking lot was meant to be the south lot, pushing fans to stroll through the training facility to get to the ballpark. In practice, most fans didn't want a leisurely stroll through the training fields and instead wanted to go directly to the ballpark, serviced by the west parking lot. So now the west parking lot is the main parking lot, and the south lot is used when there is a large crowd expected. If you want the full spring-training experience, park in the south (Camelback Road) dirt parking lot and walk in through the complex. Personally, we prefer the long stroll through the training camp—but we understand if you don't. As a bonus: Last spring parking was free.

INSIDER'S TIP

When a large crowd is expected, fans will be directed to the south lot, resulting in some long lines in the right-hand lane. Zip around them in the left lane and head to Ball Park Boulevard. Hang a right and head to the west parking-lot entrances, where there will almost certainly be shorter lines.

INSIDER'S TIP

There are ticket windows located off both main entrances. You can pick up Will Call tickets at any window.

Where to Sit

Virtually every seat in Camelback Ranch–Glendale is in the sun. Because of the grandstand orientation, fans in the grandstand are facing southeast, as opposed to the traditional northeast. That cuts down on opportunities for shade. Bring sunscreen or buy some in a team store. As a plus, there are no bleachers at Camelback Ranch–Glendale: every seat is a stadium-style seat.

Still, there are some shaded seats. The second-level overhang extends to cover much of Sections 110-117 as well as the very last rows of other nearby 100-level sections.

INSIDER'S TIP

Sections are numbered clockwise, beginning in the right-field corner and extended to the left-field corner. To sit near the White Sox dugout, go for Sections 5-11; to sit near the Dodgers dugout, go for Sections 19-25. For a great view of the South Mountains, sit on the third-base side.

INSIDER'S TIP

The Legends Deck is sold as a group space. If it is not taken by a group, it's available as a game-day purchase. It's a fully shaded area with comfortable seating.

Camelback Ranch–Glendale sports one of the largest berm areas in all of baseball, easily accommodating 3,000 folks. On a typical sunny afternoon, your best bet is sitting in the left-field area: you won't be staring into the sun. But there will be a drawback to some berm seating: you won't be able to see the right-center scoreboard. Camelback Ranch–Glendale could definitely use some more signage when it comes to scores, stats, and other graphics. It could also use some cupholders: only sections 14 and 15 contain seats with cupholders.

INSIDER'S TIP

If you are there with a group of three or four, head for one of the high tops past the berm and claim one for the day. If you're there by yourself and want a place to hang out, we recommend two SRO areas: on the concourse behind home plate (in the shade, natch) or in the left-field berm, where a drink rail was installed behind the Dodgers bullpen.

One other huge plus for Camelback Ranch–Glendale: it is one of the most accessible ballparks in all of spring training. Everyone enters at ground level, and there's an accessible ramp located down the third-base line next to section 128 for those needing to get to lower areas of seating. ADA seating is located throughout the concourse, including platforms above sections 3, 4, 11, 15, 26, 27, 102, 103, 104, 106, 107, 108 (if not used by a TV crew), 112, 118, 121, 123 (if not used by a TV crew), 124, 126, 127, and 128.

Some fans love sitting near the bullpens. For your planning purposes: the Dodgers bullpen is in the left-field corner in front of the berm, the White Sox bullpen is in the right-field corner in front of the berm. You can get close to the White Sox bullpen from the berm—handy for autograph begging before and after the game—but the berm layout keeps fans a fair distance away from the Dodgers bullpen. As a bonus, both bullpens now sport the retired numbers of players.

Selfie Spots

The life-size Tommy Lasorda bobblehead has proven to be a big
hit with the fans, as is the signpost on the Dodgers side with distance and directions to the team's minor-league affiliates.

If You Go

What to Do Outside the Ballpark

Development was supposed to accompany the ballpark, but the
bad economy scared off investors, so the ballpark is somewhat of
an island in Glendale. There is not much within walking distance
of the ballpark yet, save lots of housing developments.

The 101/Camelback interchange features a slew of fast-food joints
of the national variety. Of course, we'd recommend the In-and-
Out Burger (*9585 W. Camelback Rd.*) or Culver's (*5127 N. 99th
Av.*) for something out of the ordinary. For a better selection of
restaurants, head north to the Glendale Avenue exit: you'll find a
Gordon Biersch brewpub (*6915 N. 95th Av.; gordonbiersch.com*)
and Yard House Glendale (*9401 W. Westgate Blvd.; yard-
house.com*), a sports bar with a long beer list. Head farther north to
Northern Avenue and you'll encounter another set of better restaurants, including a Fleming's Steakhouse (*9712 W. Northern Av.,
flemingssteakhouse.com*) and a Grimaldi's Pizzeria (*9788 W.
Northern Av.; Peoria; grimaldispizzeria.com*).

Where to Stay

There is no hotel near the ballpark. The closest hotel is a Comfort
Suites near the 101 loop (*9824 W. Camelback Rd., Glendale;
623-271-9005; comfortsuites.com*), over a mile away. The official
White Sox hotel in 2015 was SpringHill Suites Glendale (*7370
North Zanjero Blvd., Glendale; 623/772-9200; marriott.com*),
while the Dodgers did not designate an official hotel in 2015.

If you want to stay relatively close to the ballpark, there are clusters of hotels near the 101/I-10 interchange (Holiday Inn Express, Quality Inn, Hilton Garden Inn, etc.) and University of Phoenix Stadium/Gila River Arena area (ranging from Hampton Inn and Staybridge Suites to Renaissance Phoenix Glendale Hotel & Spa). These are chain hotels at various price points, but there is an abundance of choices.

Within a short drive is a classic Valley of the Sun resort, the Wigwam Resort and Spa. Built on a former Goodyear cotton farm, the resort opened in 1929 with enough rooms for 24 guests. Over the years the emphasis changed to golf and spa living, and in that time the area around the resort morphed from open country to suburbia. A part of that 1929 building is still in use as a reminder of the resort's past. *Wigwam Resort and Spa, 300 Wigwam Boulevard, Litchfield Park; 800/327-0396; wigwamresort.com.*

Spring-Training History: Chicago White Sox

The Chicago White Sox have held spring training in Excelsior Springs, Mo. (1901-1902); Mobile (1903); Marlin, Texas (1904); New Orleans (1905-1906); Mexico City (1907); Los Angeles (1908); San Francisco (1909-1910); Mineral Wells, Texas (1911, 1916-1919); Waco, Texas (1912, 1920); Paso Robles, Cal. (1913-1915); Waxahachie, Texas (1921); Seguin, Texas (1922-1923); Winter Haven, Fla. (1924); Shreveport, La. (1925-1928); Dallas (1929); San Antonio (1930-1932); Pasadena, Cal. (1933-1942, 1946-1950); French Lick, Ind. (1943-1944); Terre Haute, Ind. (1945); Palm Springs, Cal. (1951); El Centro, Cal. (1952-1953); Tampa (1954-1959); Sarasota (1960-1997); Tucson (1998-2010); and Glendale, Az. (2011-present).

Spring-Training History: Los Angeles Dodgers

The Los Angeles Dodgers have trained in the following locations:

Charlotte, N.C. (1901); Columbia, S.C. (1902-1906); Jacksonville
(1907-1909); Hot Springs, Ark. (1910-1912); Augusta, Ga.
(1913-1914); Daytona Beach (1915-1916); Hot Springs, Ark.
(1917-1918); Jacksonville (1919-1920); New Orleans (1921);
Jacksonville (1922); Clearwater (1923-1932); Miami (1933);
Orlando (1934-1935); Clearwater (1936-1940); Havana
(1941-1942); Bear Mountain, N.Y. (1943-1945); Daytona Beach
(1946); Havana (1947); Ciudad Trujillo, Dominican Republic
(1948); Vero Beach (1949-2008); Phoenix (2008); and Glendale
(2009-present).

A Final Nod to Dodgertown

It's impossible to write about Dodgers spring training and not discuss the team's longtime Florida home, Vero Beach's Dodgertown.

With the Dodgers as a tenant, Dodgertown was the most historic
venues in spring-training history. Walking through the grounds of
Dodgertown was a timeless experience: you were likely to run into
the likes of Tommy Lasorda or Sandy Koufax checking out the
latest phenoms, while the ghosts of Don Drysdale and Walter
Alston hung back in the shadows. The place didn't change much
in the last 50 years—which was both a good thing and a bad thing.

The Dodgers were attracted to the area by Bud Holman, a local
entrepreneur and director of Eastern Air Lines. He persuaded
Buzzy Bavasi (then the farm director of the Brooklyn Dodgers) to
consolidate spring training for the Dodgers and their 30-plus farm
teams. The city of Vero Beach wasn't sure this was a good
idea—as a matter of fact, the city refused to put in a swimming
pool that Holman requested—so technically the Dodgers con-
tracted with Holman, who in turn leased the land from the city.

The Dodgers were so pleased with spring training in Vero Beach
that by 1952 the Dodgers signed a 21-year lease with the city for a

true Dodgertown at a former Naval air base. As part of the lease, the Dodgers agreed that the entire major-league club and 50 percent of the Dodgers' farm teams would train in Vero Beach. The players were put up in former Naval barracks.

The Dodgers then furthered their commitment a few months later by investing $100,000 in a new ballpark, named Holman Stadium, with 1,500 steel chairs brought from Ebbets Field in Brooklyn. Holman Stadium has an impressive lineage: it was designed by Norman Bel Geddes (designer of the Futurama building at the 1964 New York World's Fair) and engineered by Captain Emil Praeger, who also engineered Dodger Stadium in Los Angeles.

In the end, the needs of the Los Angeles Dodgers were different than the needs of the Brooklyn Dodgers. Even when the team moved to Los Angeles, Brooklyn fans made the familiar trip to Dodgertown. But as these fans died out, they weren't replaced by Los Angelinos, and crowds shrunk for spring training. The Dodgers attempted to shift spring training to Arizona several times before successfully working out a Camelback Ranch deal, and despite the many fond memories of training in Florida, it made sense for the Los Angeles Dodgers to take up spring residence closer to the team's fan base.

GOODYEAR BALLPARK / CINCINNATI REDS / CLEVELAND INDIANS

QUICK FACTS

- **Capacity**: 10,311
- **Year Opened**: 2009
- **Dimensions**: 345L, 380LC, 410C, 380R, 345R
- **Dugout Locations**: Reds on the third-base side, Indians on the first-base side
- **Practice Times**: Gates open at 9 a.m., with practices starting at 9:30 a.m.
- **Gates Open**: 90 minutes before game time. Home batting practice, 10:15-11:15 a.m. at complex; visitors batting practice, 11:15 a.m.-12:15 p.m.; visitors infield, 12:15-12:25 p.m. Add six hours for a night game.
- **Ticket Lines**: 800/745-3000, 866/488-7423 (Indians), 623/882-3130 (Reds)
- **Address**: 1933 S. Ballpark Way, Goodyear, AZ 85338

- **Directions**: From Downtown Phoenix/East Valley: West on I-10 to Exit 127, Bullard Avenue and proceed south (left off exit). Bullard Avenue will turn into West Lower Buckeye Road. Stay to the right and turn right on to Wood Boulevard. From West Phoenix/Surface streets route: South on Litchfield Road to Van Buren. West on Van Buren to Bullard Avenue. South on Bullard Avenue, which will become West Lower Buckeye Road. Stay to the right and turn right on to Wood Boulevard.

A Little Bit of Ohio in the Desert

When the Cleveland Indians returned in 2009 for a second stint in the Arizona League, it was a return to roots: the Indians and the New York Giants comprised the beginnings of the modern-day Cactus League, so to speak, when Bill Veeck wanted spring operations closer to his ranch in the Tucson area and made arrangements accordingly.

And when the Cincinnati Reds arrived in 2010, it made for a

unique all-Ohio training complex. There's no other two-team
training complex where the two teams are from the same state.
Geography usually breeds competitive juices; one can't imagine
the Dodgers and Angels sharing a complex, or the Mets and Yankees sharing facilities. But it works here, where Ohio roots run
deep.

There are plenty of ties between Ohio, Goodyear, and Goodyear
Ballpark aside from baseball. In 1917, the Goodyear Tire and Rub-
ber Company, still headquartered in Ohio, purchased 16,000 acres
of land that makes up part of modern Goodyear. It was an agricultural investment: the land was used to grow cotton, and Goodyear
used that cotton to make airplane tires during World War I.

The land was chiefly agricultural and rural, but in 1946 the town
of Goodyear was incorporated, complete with 151 homes and a
grocery store. World War II provided a financial lift to the city
after the Litchfield Naval Air Facility and the Goodyear Aircraft
Corporation was located there, with blimps and Navy Blue Angels
the order of the day. The facility ended up being converted to
Phoenix Goodyear Airport, located directly east of the ballpark;
it's still used as a freight airport and a storage area for grounded
planes, easily seen from the upper floors of the grandstand.

When Goodyear Ballpark was first presented to city officials, it
was envisioned as the centerpiece of a larger downtown-style
complex that included retail, office space, and hotels. But the economic turndown caused problems for the developer, and as a result
the associated development did not take place. That's why there's
so much open land next to the ballpark; the downtown-style development was envisioned both south and north of the ballpark.

Unfortunately, it now feels a little like the ballpark is sitting in the
middle of nowhere, and for good reason: It is. That's a shame,
because Goodyear Ballpark is a nice, simple little facility with a
unique industrial finish. The training facilities for the Indians and

Reds sit south of the ballpark on South Wood Boulevard and represent state-of-the-art spring training and rehab facilities.

INSIDER'S TIP
If you're heading to practice fields and not the main ballpark, you'll want to plug some slightly different addresses into the GPS. The Indians workout facility is located at 2601 S. Wood Boulevard, while the Reds training facility is at 3125 S. Wood Boulevard. Each training complex has six full practice fields and two half fields. The two fields to the north of each complex are designated for use solely by the teams; the four cloverleaf fields are at the disposal of Goodyear for youth and adult baseball.

There are some unique touches to the ballpark. First, clubhouses are located in a building in right field topped by the Right Field Pavilion concessions area. Players enter the ballpark from right-field doors. As we noted, the finishes throughout—ranging from the grandstand to the outfield building and concession booths—are consistent, with an industrial finish throughout.

History is represented at the ballpark. An exhibition from the Play Ball Experience, devoted to Cactus League history, can be found in the entry area, across from the Team Store. Right inside the home-plate gates you'll find the Ohio Cup, awarded to the team that wins the annual interleague series between the teams.

INSIDER'S TIP
No matter where you park, walk to the ballpark and enter through the home-plate gate. You'll get a good look at the baseball sculpture, The Ziz, from noted artist Donald Lipski. Measuring 60 feet, 6 inches, the 6,000-point sculpture combines some baseball elements (baseball seams) into a stylized and striking focal point for the ballpark. It cost the city of Goodyear $450,000.

INSIDER'S TIP

One thing that distinguishes the Goodyear Ballpark game-
day experience: live organ music, which is somewhat of an
endangered species in any spring-training ballpark.

Sadly, it's taken some time for Cincinnati Reds fans to discover
what a good experience can be had in Arizona, and neither team is
a good draw. Maybe it's the distance (Cincy to Sarasota is drivable
on a very long day; Cincy to Goodyear is a 27-hour drive) or the
expensive airfares, but Reds fans have not turned out to support
their team in spring training: attendance is down since the Reds
shifted spring operations to Florida (90,489 in 2008, 64,228 in
2015). The opposite is true for the Indians: spring attendance was
71,593 during the team's last spring in Winter Haven and 85,874
in 2015. While Indians attendance has increased, Reds attendance
is static. Which is good news for you: smaller crowds means a better choice of tickets, as plenty of good seats can be found when
walking up to the gate.

Things are run in Goodyear pretty much the way the Indians and
Reds ran things in Florida: low-key, with an emphasis on the
game. (Although Goodyear Ballpark is also notable for something
else: its own mascot, Zizzy.) The remote location may scare some
spring-training fans from making the trip to Goodyear, but don't
be deterred: Goodyear Ballpark is an underrated facility and worth
the drive.

INSIDER'S TIP

We can't walk the Goodyear Ballpark concourse without
remembering Indians Hall of Famer Bob Feller, who traditionally set up a table by the front entrance—wherever the
Indians were training—and sold autographs. He also threw
out the first pitch here. His presence is felt years after his
death.

It's taken a little longer than expected for Goodyear Ballpark to
generate any momentum. The general area around the ballpark is a

mix of planned communities (to the west), agricultural land (to the north), the airport and Avondale (to the east), and Estrella Mountain to the south. Until development spruces up the area, you'll need to be happy with just a baseball game during a trip to Goodyear Ballpark—but that's certainly not the worst thing in the world.

The Spring-Training Ballpark Experience

Concessions

Concessions were overhauled in 2016, with a new concessionaire in place. A new group of specialty stands are now in the concourse, with three stands in the grandstand (two food and beer, one beer and cocktails) still in place. You can find a wide variety of hot dots, top-notch brats, burgers, and other ballpark fare at these stands, but we'd recommending heading to the specialty stands for something unique.

> **INSIDER'S TIP**
> Yes, Cincinnati fans, there is Skyline Chili for your hot dogs.

For instance, there's a separate Philly cheesesteak stand behind home plate worth a stop, and a Baskin-Robins ice-cream stand down the first-base line. Other new specialty booths feature barbeque, fry bread, and smokies. And, as you'll find in many spring-training ballparks, the food offerings are spiced up with the presence of food trucks.

One thing new with the concessionaire change: an expansion of beer offerings. Most are of the MillerCoors variety, along with some indies and import offerings like Dale's Pale Ale, Pabst Blue Ribbon (in the obligatory tallboy), and Heineken. A local favorite, SanTan Devil's Ale, is on tap as well.

> **INSIDER'S TIP**

The $32 Right Field Pavilion serves an all-you-can-eat buffet meal and offers some nice seating. If you arrive hungry at the ballpark, we'd recommend it.

INSIDER'S TIP
You can bring in a single unopened water bottle and unopened snacks (chips, peanuts, etc.). You cannot bring in prepared food in your own container.

Autographs

Generally speaking, this is a poor place to snare an autograph. There's no dedicated or traditional signing spot, and with the players entering and leaving from a right-field clubhouse, there's little chance for anyone to stop and sign in the midst of a game. Your best chance for an autograph—besides batting practices, of course—is to hope a player will come out to sign at some point down the line.

Parking

You won't have much choice other than to pay $5 for access to the lots. When a big crowd is expected, ballpark officials will send out carts to help those with physical challenges more easily reach the front gates. There is limited street parking in the area, but you'll find it to be quite a hike from these spots to the ballpark. One tip: The ballpark is close enough to the training complexes that you can hit the morning practices and then walk over for the 1:05 p.m. game.

INSIDER'S TIP
People sometimes complain that parking is on a grassy field and not a paved parking lot. But most folks don't realize that for the remaining 11 months of the year we're not taking about a parking lot: we are talking about youth soccer fields.

And those soccer fields provide a vital role in year-round youth activities.

For the Kids

The Kids Zone is located in the right-field corner and features standard ballpark inflatable games. In addition, there's a small wiffle-ball diamond—complete with smaller backstop—for the kids within the ballpark fence.

Where to Sit

There are no bleachers in the ballpark—only 8,007 theater-style seats. And they're mostly pretty good, except for a few clunkers. For instance, stay away from Section 105: you'll be sitting in back of a distracting tarp.

> **INSIDER'S TIP**
> Section numbering begins with 101 in the left-field corner and runs through 123 in the right-field corner. The concourse is in the back of the seating area, so no aisle runs through the seating bowl.

> **INSIDER'S TIP**
> To sit near the Reds dugout on the third-base side, buy a ticket in Sections 106-110. To sit near the Indians dugout on the first-base side, buy a ticket in Sections 114-118.

The berm isn't as large as found in other spring ballparks: it seats only 1,530, and we find it's rarely crowded. Maybe it's because there's only a little bit of prime berm area: the bullpens are beyond the home-run fence (Indians to the left, Reds to the right) and occupy areas that normally would be swarmed by fans. Similarly, the Right Field Pavilion and clubhouse takes up a lot of prime space in right field from the power alley to the foul pole. And there's one big disadvantage to sitting on the berm: you can't see the scoreboard, and there's no display on the grandstand.

If you seek shade, go for Sections 110-114, as they're protected from the sun by the press box and suites, which are built up high. Better yet, go for a ticket in the Club seating (106A, 106B, 107A): the seats are totally shaded and feature padded seats. Like many spring-training ballparks, there is free sunscreen, with dispensers next to the restrooms.

The rooftop Terrace ticket is expensive ($17), but so worth it: you can see for miles, and your views of the game are framed by Estrella Mountain to the south and the White Tank Mountains to the northwest. There are concessions, so you won't need to leave to snare a beer and a dog. The risk: tickets to the Terrace are sold only on game day, and they do sell out.

INSIDER'S TIP
Head to the center-field pub patio for some beer and shade. You can sit there if you buy a cheap berm ticket. You won't be able to see the scorebard, but then again, on a warmer late-March day, you'll appreciate the shade more.

Selfie Spot

The aforementioned Ziz sculpture outside the ballpark is by far the best spot for a selfie at Goodyear Ballpark.

What to Do Outside the Ballpark

The southwest corner of Phoenix—especially the communities along I-10, including Goodyear and Avondale—tend to be dominated by planned communities, big-box retailers, and plenty of chain developments. Not that there's anything wrong with that, but you don't travel hundreds of miles to do what you can do at home.

So your choice is simple: stay in the area and make the best of things, or hunker down in Phoenix or a more centrally located area and drive out to games.

Sticking around is actually made easier these days by the general growth in the area, particularly north of the freeway. There are two sports bars worth your attention.

Augie's Sports Grill is a good destination during March Madness, with multiple TV screens providing the action. The food is strictly pub grub, but the drinks are cheap (particularly during Happy

Hour, which runs through 7 p.m.). *Augie's Sports Grill, 15605 W. Roosevelt St., Goodyear; 623/932-0001; augiessportsgrill.com.*

We already discussed Dan Majerle and his downtown Phoenix sports bar, but he's opened another in Goodyear and is within a few miles of Goodyear Ballpark. Same menu as the downtown sports bar, same good beer list. *Majerle's Sports Bar, 13375 W. McDowell Rd., Goodyear; 623/207-6999; majerles.com.*

If you choose to stay in Goodyear, check out the Wigwam Golf Resort & Spa (*300 E. Wigwam Blvd., Litchfield Park, 623/ 935-3811; wigwamresort.com*), a 400-acre, 331-room complex with three 18-hole championship courses. The resort dates back to 1929, but has been seriously upgraded in recent years. The Wigwam Bar, with its indoor/outdoor seating, is definitely a draw.

Where to Stay

There are no hotels within walking distance of the ballpark, but there are plenty as you get close to I-10. The official hotel for the Reds is the Marriott Residence Inn (*7350 N. Zanjero Blvd., Glendale; 623/772-8900; marriott.com*). The Indians do not designate an official hotel for major leaguers, but do for the minor league players: Quality Inn & Suites (*950 N. Dysart, Glendale; 623/ 932-9191; choicehotels.com*). Other hotels within a close drive include Hampton Inn and Suites (*2000 N. Litchfield Rd., Goodyear; 623/536-1313; hilton.com*), Holiday Inn Express (*1313 N. Litchfield Rd., Goodyear; 623/535-1313; holiday-inn.com*), TownPlace Suites (*13971 W. Celebrate Life Way, Goodyear; 623/ 535-5009; marriott.com*), and Holiday Inn & Suites (*1188 N. Dysart Rd., Goodyear; 623/547-1313; holiday-inn.com*).

Spring-Training History: Cincinnati Reds

The Cincinnati Reds have trained in the following locations: Cincinnati (1901-1902); Augusta, Ga. (1903); Dallas (1904); Jacksonville (1905); San Antonio (1906); Marlin Springs, Texas (1907); St. Augustine (1908); Atlanta (1909); Hot Springs, Ark. (1910-1911); Columbus, Ga. (1912); Mobile, Ala. (1913); Alexandria, La. (1914-1915); Shreveport (1916-1917); Montgomery, Ala. (1918); Waxahachie, Texas (1919); Miami (1920); Cisco, Texas (1921); Mineral Wells, Texas (1922); Orlando (1923-1930); Tampa (1931-1942); Bloomington, Ind. (1943-1945); Tampa (1946-1987); Plant City, Fla. (1988-1997); Sarasota (1998-2009); and Goodyear (2010-present).

The ballparks used by the Reds in Sarasota (Ed Smith Stadium) and Plant City (Plant City Stadium) still stand. Ed Smith Stadium has been renovated and is now spring home of the Baltimore Orioles, while Plant City Stadium is home to the International Softball Federation after undergoing a 1999 renovation.

Spring-Training History: Cleveland Indians

The Cleveland Indians have trained in the following locations:
Cleveland (1901); New Orleans (1902-1903); San Antonio (1904);
Atlanta (1905-1906); Macon, Ga. (1907-1908); Mobile, Ala.
(1909); Alexandria, La. (1910-1911); Mobile, Ala. (1912); Pensacola, Fla. (1913); Athens, Ga. (1914); San Antonio (1915); New
Orleans (1916-1920); Dallas (1921-1922); Lakeland (1923-1927);
New Orleans (1928-1939); Ft. Myers (1940-1941); Clearwater
(1942); Lafayette, Ind. (1943-1945); Clearwater (1946); Tucson
(1947-1992); Winter Haven (1993-2008); and Goodyear
(2009-present).

Many of the former spring homes of the Indians still stand.
Despite being slated at one point for redevelopment, Chain of
Lakes Park in Winter Haven, as well as the old training fields, are
still in use, mostly for youth baseball tournaments. Hi Corbett
Field, the team's original Cactus League home, is still is use as
home of the University of Arizona Wildcats baseball team.

HOHOKAM STADIUM / OAKLAND ATHLETICS

QUICK FACTS

- **Capacity**: 10,000
- **Year Opened**: 1997; renovated 2015
- **Dimensions**: 340L, 385LC, 411C, 385RC, 350R
- **Dugout Location**: First-base side
- **Practice Times**: Practices begin at 10 a.m. at Fitch Park (160 E. 6th Place, Mesa)
- **Gates Open**: Grandstand opens two hours before game time. Athletics batting practice, until 11 a.m.; visitors batting practice, 11 a.m.-noon; Athletics infield, 12-12:10 p.m.; visitors infield, 12:10-12:20 p.m.
- **Ticket Line**: 480/907-5489
- **Address**: 1235 N. Center St., Mesa 85201
- **Directions**: From Phoenix, take 202 Loop east to exit 12 (McKellips Road), turn right on W. McKellips Road; and turn right onto N. Center Street. Hohokam Stadium will be on the left-hand side of the street.

Back to the Future in Mesa

Now one of the most pleasant experiences in the Cactus League,
an Oakland Athletics game at Mesa's Hohokam Stadium is a must
for anyone craving a low-key spring-training match.

Hohokam Stadium was originally built in 1977, rebuilt in 1997 for
the Chicago Cubs, and then upgraded yet again for the 2015
arrival of the Athletics. (It opened as Hohokam Park per a concourse plaque, but somehow acquired the Hohokam Stadium
name.) Every trace of the Cubbie red and blue was removed from
Hohokam Stadium, as the A's and Mesa forged a new identity.
The ballpark was changed in several different ways, all enhancing
the fan experience. If you were a Cubs fan who spent a lot of time
at Hohokam Park, the new Hohokam is recognizable—but just
barely.

First, a layer of green-and-gold paint—as well as lots of
grey—replaced the Cubs red and blue. Second, the ballpark's
capacity is smaller—just 10,000, down from the 12,575 capacity

when the Cubs were in town, as some seating was removed to make way for party decks, complete with their own concessions, picnic tables, and drink rails on the home side. (The away side sports artificial turf and no drink rails.) While these drink rails were a little too off the action to be usable for most of the game, they still attract plenty of fans. Perhaps the best thing about both party decks: they are shaded. Third, the A's and Mesa installed the largest videoboard in all of spring training, providing crystal-clear replays, player shots, and more to A's fans. The Daktronics high-def videoboard, measuring 56 feet wide and 32 feet tall, is bright and clearly visible from every part of the ballpark—except for the folks sitting on the berm in the left-field corner. (So don't sit there.) For players, an expanded clubhouse with new weight room provides more comfort than experienced at Phoenix Municipal Stadium. And then there's the Lew Wolff Training Center at Fitch Park, which raises Athletics training abilities to a new level.

INSIDER'S TIP

The Athletics do not practice at Hohokam Stadium during the practice portion of training camp, before games begin. Instead, the Athletics practice at Lew Wolff Training Center at Fitch Park (655 N. Center St.), just up the road from Hohokam Stadium. Practices begin at 10 a.m., with the major-league squad dressing at Hohokam Stadium and then transported down to Fitch Park. Access to players at Fitch Park is decent, as fans are directed to seating and standing-room areas in the middle of the field.

There are four fields at Fitch Park, and they're all used in spring training. They also feature bleacher seating, as well as a concessions stand.

The ballpark is closest to sacred ground in the Cactus League. The site housed the original Rendezvous Park, which dates back to 1921 as a baseball field; it became a spring-training site when the Cubs began their first spring-training tenancy there in 1952. This

is actually the second Hohokam Stadium. The first was built in
1976 as the spring-training home of the Athletics, who quickly
bailed on Mesa and made way for the Cubs to return in 1979.

The Spring-Training Ballpark Experience

Concessions

Spectra (formerly Ovations) is still in charge of the food at
Hohokam Stadium, but they couldn't address one of the big problems with the ballpark: with a 1970s design, most concession
stands are under the grandstand, in a concourse with no view of
the action. There are some Oakland touches to the proceedings—the popular Ike's Love & Sandwiches, an Oakland institution with a Tempe outpost, attracts some long lines—and there
were hot dogs pitched as Oakland favorites. (The Oakland Dog,
with mac and cheese, chilies and bacon, is especially tasty, as is
the freshly made corn dog.) Burger Prime is a popular spot, with
good reason: the offerings are great. And, like most other spring-
training venues, the Coliseum is now home to plenty of food
trucks.

But few local brews are on tap, save the offerings at a Lagunitas
Brewing Company stand on the home side (though Four Peaks
could be found in a can), and a standard array of the usual suspects
($7 for a domestic like Bud, $9 for a tall boy or a premium like
Goose Island) were featured throughout the ballpark. At the end of
the Cubs' tenure, there was a big emphasis on booze at the ballpark; that emphasis is gone, for the better.

Autographs

Players will usually hang out before the game in front of the tarp
next to the home dugout down the first-base line. You can also
hang around Fitch Park (655 N. Center St.) and hit morning prac-

tices, which begin at 9:30 a.m. Otherwise, it's hard to snare an autograph at Hohokam Stadium.

Parking

There is adequate paid parking next to the ballpark: 3,000 spots, give or take. The cost is a reasonable $5—cheaper than when the Cubs were in town. Interestingly, there's not as much tailgating before the game as you might expect.

Many fans drive into the surrounding neighborhood to park for free or with a homeowner. These spots go for $5 or so. Beware: Mesa law authorities rigorously enforce the signs warning against ballgame parking.

Getting into the ballpark is no great shakes: there are long lines if you're coming from the north on Center Street. Our advice is to loop to the south of the ballpark and make your way north on Center Street. You may also snare some street parking if you arrive early enough. One spot where the parking is free: Brown Road, south of the ballpark, where you'll find crowds parking for free and walking the short distance to Hohokam Stadium.

Where to Sit

With the changes, there's now an abundance of shade at Hohokam Stadium, thanks to a new canopy covering much of the grandstand. That means a very large share of the 200-level seating—basically, anything from Section 202 on the third-base side down to Section 213—is now fully shaded at the start of the game. (If you sit in the closer 100-level seats, you'll be in the sun. Bring sunscreen, as there are no sunscreen dispensers as found in other spring-training ballparks.) There's also shade in the upper-level group picnic areas.

If your only choice is between seats far down the line or the berm, go for the berm, still one of the great areas in spring training. It's easily accessible via a center-field entrance (close to much of the parking), it has its own concessions, and it's still the venue for hardcore fans. A warning: The berm can be a serious sun field on a hot day (in other words, bring your sunscreen).

INSIDER'S TIP
Hohokam Stadium seat numbers follow the even/odd convention: even numbers to the left of home plate and odd numbers to the right. When you have a choice, sit in an odd-numbered section.

INSIDER'S TIP
If you get to the berm early, stake out a spot in right field. Both bullpens are located there beyond the home-run fence, and fans can sit right next to the pens. The A's bullpen is closest to the playing field.

INSIDER'S TIP
Sit in an even-numbered seat if you want a great back-drop—the Superstition Mountains—to the action.

INSIDER'S TIP
The Hyatt Place Patio is a reserved covered area above Terrace Box sections 210/212 for guests to enjoy a catered meal and a game.

Selfie Spot

Sadly, there's not really a great selfie spot at Hohokam Stadium. You will see folks head down behind the dugouts for a selfie, but the A's need to put up a 10-foot-high logo somewhere in the concourse to foster those spring selfies.

If You Go

Where to Stay

Mesa does feel like it is a separate area of the Phoenix region, and if you're a true A's fan you'll want to spend as much time as possible hanging around the ballpark and practice facility. There are a number of hotels within two miles of the ballpark:

- Phoenix Mesa Marriott, 200 N. Centennial Way, Mesa; 480/898-8300; *marriott.com*. Technically, this is the hotel closest to the ballpark.
- Mesa Mezona Inn, 250 W. Main St., Mesa; 480/834-9233; *bestwestern.com*. We'd highly recommend the Mezona Inn; it's a traditional hot spot during spring training.
- Hyatt Place Phoenix/Mesa, W. Bass Pro Dr., Mesa; 480/969-8200; *hyatt.com*. This hotel is also close to Sloan Park, home of the Cubs, making it a good central base for spring training.
- Baymont Inn & Suites Mesa, 651 E. Main St., Mesa; 480/621-6375; *wyndhamhotels.com*.

The official team hotel in 2016 was the Doubletree Suites Hotel (*320 N. 44th St., Phoenix; 602/225-0500; hilton.com*).

RV Resorts Near the Ballpark

The ballpark is in the western part of Mesa, putting it a decent distance from the many RV parks in eastern Mesa and Apache Junction.

And there is an abundance of them, to be sure. Mesa is known in some circles as being the RV park center of the Phoenix area. That's not necessarily a bad thing. There are at least 16 RV parks in the greater Mesa area, and that's not counting more in Tempe,

Gilbert, Chandler, and Apache Junction. Check out the likes of
Tower Point or Good Life (*cal-am.com*), and Mesa Spirit
(*mesaspirit.com*), but be warned that in general the RV resorts in
Mesa are really snowbird camps.

Nearby Restaurants

If you liked Ike's at Hohokam Stadium, you'll love it at a Mesa
location. Oakland fans will feel right at home with Pat Tillman and
Reading Rainbow subs, along with ingredients like chicken-fried
steak. *Ike's Place, 1130 W. Grove Av., Suite 110, Mesa; 480/
610-6750; ilikeikesplace.com.*

A Mexican mainstay in the general area is Serrano's Mexican
Food, with several locations throughout the Valley. The Serrano
family has been in business in Arizona since 1919, but at that time
the family business was clothing. In 1979 the Serrano family
ditched the clothing and shifted into the Mexican restaurant business, keeping the Serrano logo. You'll find the usual Mexican fare
at Serrano's, though there's a noted emphasis on seafood dishes
like *pescado a la tortilla* (tilapia encrusted with tortilla) and *enchiladas de camaron* (shrimp enchiladas). *Serrano's Fine Mexican
Food, 1964 E. McKellips Rd., Mesa; 480/649-3503; serra-
nosaz.com.*

The ballpark is north of downtown Mesa; while other communities
in the Valley of the Sun are forced to create downtowns from
scratch, Mesa has a historic one. Downtown Mesa has its own historic districts and attractions; you could do worse than spending
some time driving around and taking in a show or exhibit at the
Mesa Arts Center (*1 E. Main St., Mesa; 480/644-6500; mesaarts-
center.com*).

If you tire of crowds, we can recommend an out-of-the-way spot
that features a huge wine and beer selection as well as a civilized
environment: Sun Devil Wine Cellar & Pub, located in the base-

ment of Sun Devil Liquors in downtown Mesa (*235 N. Country Club Dr., 480/834-5050, sundevilliquors.com*). It's a small place, but features live music on Thursdays and Saturdays.

Spring-Training History: Oakland Athletics

Oakland Athletics spring-training sites have included: Philadelphia (1901, 1919); Charlotte, N.C. (1902); Jacksonville (1903, 1914-1918); Spartanburg, S.C. (1904); Shreveport (1905); Montgomery, Ala. (1906, 1923-1924); Dallas (1907); New Orleans (1908-1909); Atlanta (1910); San Antonio (1912-1913); Lake Charles, La. (1920-1921, 1938-1939); Eagle Pass, Texas (1922); Ft. Myers (1925-1936); Mexico City (1937); Anaheim, Cal. (1940-1942); Wilmington, Del. (1943); Frederick, Md. (1944-1945); West Palm Beach (1946-1962); Bradenton (1963-1969); Mesa (1969-1978; 2015-present); Scottsdale (1979-1983); Phoenix (1984-2014).

MARYVALE BASEBALL PARK / MILWAUKEE BREWERS

QUICK FACTS

- **Capacity**: 7,000, plus berm seating
- **Year Opened**: 1998
- **Dimensions**: 350L, 400C, 340R
- **Dugout Location**: First-base side
- **Practice Times**: Gates open at 7 a.m., but practices don't start until 9:30 a.m.
- **Gates Open**: Two hours before game time, but don't be surprised if you arrive at the ballpark and the gates aren't opened or they've been open for a half hour; the Brewers are notoriously casual about these things. Brewers BP and infield, 10-11:15 a.m.; visitors BP and infield, 11:15 a.m.-12:15 p.m.
- **Ticket Line**: 800/933-7890
- **Address**: 3600 N. 51st Av., Phoenix, AZ 85031
- **Directions**: Take 51st Avenue (Exit 139 off I-10) north

for two miles. Maryvale Baseball Park is on the left past Thomas Road and just before Indian School Road.

Maryvale: Far from the Madding Crowds

Hate crowds? Want to feel close to your favorite ballplayer, even if they don't play for the Brew Crew? Then look no further than Maryvale Baseball Park, the spring-training home of the Milwaukee Brewers, which has been largely unchanged in recent years. The Brewers front office hasn't been shy about expressing a desire for a new training facility in the Cactus League, but with efforts stalled—those with the will lack the money, those with the money lack the will—it looks like the Brewers will be at Maryvale Baseball Park for the foreseeable future.

This ballpark is the great secret of Cactus League spring training: since the Brewers don't draw very well on their own, there are usually good tickets available for almost every spring-training tilt. That's why fans of visiting teams can outnumber Brewers fans for games against popular teams like the Cubbies or the Giants. And at a time when Cactus League ballparks have been modernized and upgraded in recent years, Maryvale Baseball Park pretty much remains the same—which is either a good thing or bad thing, depending on your point of view.

And no matter where your team allegiances lie, you'll find Maryvale Baseball Park to be a very pleasant place to take in a baseball game. Despite its name, the training complex is actually within Phoenix city limits; Maryvale is a neighborhood in western Phoenix, bumping up against Glendale. It is a spacious ballpark, designed to accommodate two teams in the spring (a la Peoria or Surprise) but housing only the Brewers. There's plenty of space surrounding the ballpark, as well as ample seating (7,000 seats, plus 1,000 or so on lawn seating) within. With the departure of the Oakland A's for Mesa, this is the only spring-training complex within Phoenix proper.

The layout should be familiar to anyone who has visited a newer ballpark in the last decade: it utilizes the familiar plan of a rear concourse with ample concessions in back of the seating area, so you're never out of view of the action. The 56-acre complex features five full major-/minor-league practice facilities, two half-field practice facilities, a major-league clubhouse, and a minor-league clubhouse. The training facility is open before home games, so feel free to wander around and see future Brewers in action.

There are some pleasant aspects to Maryvale Baseball Park. As noted, there's a lot of shade in the ballpark: a canopy runs from third base to the right-field corner, with smaller canopies running down the left-field line. The concessions from Delaware North are good, if not limited: there is a good beer selection (Miller brews, of course, including Miller High Life), and a concourse area featuring grills with burgers, brats, and chicken tenders. The main concession stands offer $5 Klements brats, chorizo and Polish sausages. And, of course, there's the mandatory Bloody Mary stand—we are talking Sconnie fans, after all.

Though pleasant, we're talking about a rather basic facility. There's no huge grandstand, no huge façade announcing you've come to the right place. You'll know you're at the front gates because of the multistory sign (sans a Brewers logo, weirdly enough), not because of the basic metal fence marking the ballpark boundary. Yes, there are some clues you're in a Brewers facility during the course of a game with the familiar Sausage Race and a traditional "Roll Out the Barrel" in the middle of the seventh. But everything at Maryvale Baseball Park is on the laid-back side, and that goes for branding efforts.

There's really nothing spectacular about the ballpark, but nothing seriously wrong, either. The left-field scoreboard is basic: balls, strikes, game info, and little more. No videoboard, no replays. If you want shade, head to the concourse; a nice roof will give you relief from the sun. Need to stretch your legs? Take a hike around the 360-degree concourse, stopping for some liquid relief at one of the standalone concession stands in the left-field corner. No matter where you sit, you have easy access to concessions and you can stretch your legs throughout the course of a long game, and most fans don't need more than that.

INSIDER'S TIP
The minor-league complex has a separate address—3805 N. 53rd Avenue—and a separate parking lot. North 53rd departs from the Phoenix grid system at Indian School Road and curves to the southwest. You can enter it either from Indian School Road or Clarendon Avenue.

To avoid the sun, sit on the first-base side or in the right-field berm. A favorite tactic is to buy a berm seat, have a couple of beers while hanging around the outfield and concourse, and then claim an unused seat (in the shade) for the remainder of the game.

If an average crowd is on hand, you can move to open seating by the fifth inning or so. But we've also gone both ways on the seating level: it's not impossible to snare good seats next to a dugout a week or so before a game. (For the record, the Brewers occupy the first-base dugout.)

In recent years the Brewers have attempted to insert some essence of Miller Park into the Maryvale Baseball Park proceedings, whether it be new food items (see below) or the Famous Racing Sausages in action during the sixth inning. They've had limited success: attendance for the Brewers during springtime remains fairly low.

And there lies the issue: Maryvale Baseball Park is perfectly pleasant because the Brewers are not a strong draw. If the Brewers started attracting larger crowds, the issues with Maryvale Baseball Park would be magnified. As of now, a larger crowd taxes the ballpark infrastructure: the parking lots already fill up quickly, the lines at the concession stands are long and move slowly, and the main entry gate can back up fast. So, ironically, the best experiences at Maryvale Baseball Park happen because the Brewers are not a strong draw—so fans need to hope the team continues to lag in the attendance standings. Many Cactus League oldtimers swear by Maryvale Baseball Park for perhaps the wrong reasons: lower ticket demand, easy access to concessions (no lines!), and a lack of crowds.

Maryvale Baseball Park is an afterthought for all but hardcore Brewers fans—but it's definitely worth a visit if your favorite team happens to be the visiting team.

The Spring-Training Ballpark Experience

Concessions

As with Miller Park, a mandatory food item is a $5 Klements

bratwurst, considered among the best in the Cactus League. Top it with sauerkraut and spiced mustard. This being the spring home of the Milwaukee Brewers, there are also several other wursts, chorizo, and dogs available, as well as BBQ pork from Bill Johnson's Big Apple and chicken-breast sandwiches. And, of course, there's Miller High Life (our fave), Miller Lite, Blue Moon, Blue Moon Wit, Killian's, and Blue Moon Peach Ale on tap, though the beer prices are on the high side (a 12-ounce premium beer runs you $8.50, while a 16-ounce Lite costs $7.50). Bombers of Corona, Pacifico, Modelo, and Heineken will run you $11.

Being a Wisconsin team, the Brewers and the team's concessionaire couldn't help but bring in a few local delicacies. Deep-fried cheese curds, a staple in many Milwaukee and Madison restaurants, were available at Maryvale Baseball Park for the first time. Also made available for the first time: Bratchos, hot chips covered in nacho cheese and slices of bratwurst.

On a hot day, a frozen banana or a shaved ice can be refreshing. Most of the concessions are located behind the grandstand, but there are stands down each line as well, where you can find exotic delicacies like Mexican fare.

Autographs

There's no designated autograph area at Maryvale Baseball Park, so your best bet is to arrive early to the ballpark and attract the attention of the players as they head from the clubhouse to the field.

One nice touch: there's definitely a relaxed vibe at Maryvale Baseball Park, a vibe that seems to infect opposing teams as well. You'll usually find both teams milling around their dugout before a game, and both coaching staffs will engage in friendly chats with fans. As an organization, the Brewers have cultivated openness

with the fans, and that attitude is certainly on display at Maryvale
Baseball Park.

The entrance to the clubhouse is down the right-field line, so players must walk in foul territory after leaving the game. This is the
place to buy a ticket and try to snare an autograph before or after
the game.

Another game plan: attend morning practice. The Brewers open
workouts at 9:30 a.m. in the adjoining practice fields. You can try
to snare a player to or from workouts. Interestingly, the practice
field directly next to the ballpark—#2, named after Hank
Aaron—is closed to spectators. The five fields devoted to minor-
league workouts (and MLB workouts before the start of Cactus
League games) are named for other former Brewer greats: Cecil
Cooper, Rollie Fingers, Paul Molitor, Don Sutton, and Robin
Yount.

INSIDER'S TIP

If the Brewers have scheduled an away game and you're
really itching for a star player's signature, head to the practice facility at 9 a.m. The gates to the ballpark are open for
batting practice, and the team allows fans to watch before the
team departs at 10 a.m.

Parking

The city really does have you by the throat when it comes to parking. Your choices are to either pay $8 to park at the complex
(there's a large grassy field between the ballpark and 51st Avenue,
with a small paved area closer to the ballpark) or take your
chances parking in the surrounding area, which presents its own
set of issues. (When there's a large crowd, you're diverted to the
nearby Wal-Mart for parking.) The advice: bite the bullet and pay
for the parking. As with Miller Park, the Brewers encourage tail-

gating, so come extra early and grab a paved spot for some Sconnie-style pregame festivities.

Where to Sit

For most games you'll have a pretty solid selection of seats. There are no bleachers at Maryvale Baseball Park; only a single level of blue chairbacks, sans cupholders. The Brewers dugout is on the first-base side between Sections 105 and 113. The visitors dugout is on the third-base side between Sections 106 and 114. If there's a real character leading the opposition—say, the amiable Joe Maddon or the intense Bruce Bochy—sitting next to the visitor dugout can be a more interesting experience.

> **INSIDER'S TIP**
> You can find the most shade in the back half of most seating sections as well as the berm in right field.

Berm seating means a relaxing time in the outfield. Both bullpens are located in the outfield-berm area, so you can get up-close and personal with both sets of relief pitchers.

Selfie Spots

As noted, there's no Brewers logo on the side of the ballpark, and very little in the ballpark to mark it as a Milwaukee outpost. Your best bet is a shot with the ballpark in the background and the Brewers logo behind home plate.

If You Go

What to Do Outside the Ballpark

Maryvale is not one of the more upscale areas of Phoenix. As a matter of fact, it's a transitional area, which is a polite way of saying that the neighborhood could go to heck in the next few years,

so chances are pretty good you won't be spending much time in
the area. Your dining and entertainment options are severely limited: there's nothing nearby save a Sizzler or Denny's. If you're a
golfer, you can get in nine or 18 holes at the nearby Maryvale Golf
Course (*5902 W. Indian School Rd.*), considered to a pretty decent
municipal course.

But you are close to Glendale and the charms of that up-and-com-
ing suburb. One of our favorite sushi joints in the Valley of the
Sun is a short drive away: Moto Sushi (*6845 N. 16th St., Phoenix;
602/263-5444; mrmotorising.com*) at the corner of 16th and Glendale. Great sushi, great selection of beer, with a 3-6:15 p.m. HPPY
HR. Head there on a Sunday afternoon after the game for cheap
sushi and $3 draft beers.

Downtown Glendale has its own attractions, and it's only four or
so miles from the ballpark. If you didn't get your fill of Klements
at the ballpark, there's a pretty decent German restaurant near the
ballpark: Haus Murphy's, which features the requisite pretzels,
sausages, kraut, and schnitzel. *Haus Murphy's, 5739 W. Glendale
Av., Glendale; 623/939-2480; hausmurphys.com.*

Also in downtown Glendale: La Piazza Al Forno, which offers an
outstanding white pizza. A change of pace from the ballpark food
dominating your diet. *La Piazza Al Forno, 5803 W. Glendale Av.,
Glendale; 623/847-3301; lapiazzaalforno.com.*

Plus, you are in the western edge of Phoenix, which means you're
close to Peoria. Check out our chapters on Peoria Stadium, Surprise Stadium, Camelback Ranch–Glendale, and Goodyear Ballpark for more information on what to do in those areas.

Where to Stay

There really is no reason to stay near Maryvale Baseball Park.
There are no attractions in the surrounding neighborhood, no hot

and trendy restaurants in the area, and no hotels within walking distance. (The Milwaukee Brewers have been openly searching for a new spring-training home, and the location of Maryvale Baseball Park is a big reason why.) You will find some hotels close to I-10 within a few miles of the ballpark (in the city's Midtown area), but we're not talking about plush and scenic resorts: we're talking Super 8, Motel 6, and Red Roof Inn, all sitting next to the freeway, to boot.

INSIDER'S TIP
There was no official hotel for 2016.

Instead, look at staying either in nearby Glendale or downtown Phoenix. (We discuss downtown hotels in the previous chapter on Phoenix.) Glendale is a suburb located north and west of the Maryvale neighborhood, between Phoenix and Peoria. It's the spring home of the Los Angeles Dodgers and Chicago White Sox. It's also home to Gila River Arena, the home of the NHL's Arizona Coyotes, as well as University of Phoenix Stadium, home of the NFL's Arizona Cardinals.

Glendale is not exactly party central, but it does have its own charms: antique lovers flock to the 90 antique shops in downtown Glendale, while anyone with a sweet tooth appreciates a tour of Cerreta Candy Company. Yes, any chocolate-factory tour is merely an excuse to devour samples at the end, and the Cerreta Candy products are worth the wait: French mints, milk and dark chocolates, caramels, truffles, crunches, and nut clusters. *Cerreta Candy Company, 5345 W. Glendale Av., Glendale; 623/930-9000; cerreta.com.*

We discuss some other hotspots in the greater Glendale area in our Camelback Ranch-Glendale chapter. There has been a lot of new development in the area—though, ironically, very little close to the ballpark itself—and staying in the general area will both give you access to some great ballparks as well as good restaurants and

accommodations in the Goodyear/Glendale/Peoria freeway corridor.

Spring Training History: Milwaukee Brewers

In fact, if there's a Major League Baseball team strongly associated with spring training—at least historically—it's the Milwaukee Brewers, literally born during the last days of spring training
in 1970. As noted, the Brewers franchise began life as the Seattle
Pilots during the 1969 season. It was a rush job: MLB had not
planned on expanding until 1972 or so, but political pressure from
Missouri politicians after Charles O. Finley fled to Oakland with
the Athletics led baseball to expand in Kansas City and Seattle
ahead of schedule. That put the Pilots playing out of Sick's Stadium, a former Minor League Baseball ballpark that opened in
1938 and had seen much better days before being hastily expanded
for the 1969 season.

Everything about that 1969 season was temporary: on Opening
Day Sick's Stadium had a capacity of 17,000 or so, and it wasn't
until June that the ballpark's capacity reached 25,420—far short of
the 30,000 capacity mandated by Major League Baseball when the
Pilots expansion franchise was awarded. The Pilots ended the season in some deep debt (owing $3.5 million to Bank of California,
$1 million to stockholders, $165,000 for Sick's Stadium lease,
$250,000 to the American League for dues, among others), and the
owners—Pacific Northwest Sports, with Dewey and Max Soriano
controlling 34 percent of the shares—sought to sell the team to
Milwaukee Brewers Baseball Club, Inc., a group led by local car
salesman Allan "Bud" Selig, a former Milwaukee Braves minority
investor who would become MLB commissioner in 1992.

That sale was opposed by the city of Seattle, King County, and a
local group seeking to keep the Pilots at Sick's Stadium. The
drama played out throughout 1970 spring training, as talk of a
team move to County Stadium dominated the headlines and dis-

tracted the players training at Tempe Diablo Stadium. MLB had already approved a move to Milwaukee, and prototype Brewers uniforms surfaced on the wires in the midst of spring training. In the end, Federal Bankruptcy Referee Sidney C. Volinn approved the sale of the Pilots to Selig and crew on March 30, 1970, just a week before the regular season began.

The Brewers, therefore, became the first and last MLB team to be born during spring training.

A part of Brewers spring-training history met the wrecking ball in 2014: Compadre Stadium, the team's home in 1986-1997, was finally torn down. The Brewers left Chandler after 1997 spring training, but Chandler did not tear down the ballpark, turning the training fields into parkland and holding events in the ballpark. But city officials never really worked to bring back spring train- ing, and so the ballpark was basically disused. When a developer approached the city to build housing on the site, city leaders jumped at the chance to expand the tax base, and Compadre Sta- dium was torn down in August 2014.

PEORIA STADIUM / SAN DIEGO PADRES / SEATTLE MARINERS

QUICK FACTS

- **Capacity**: 12,393 (includes 3,000 berm seats)
- **Year Opened**: 1994
- **Dimensions**: 340L, 385LC, 410C, 385RC, 340R
- **Dugout Locations**: Mariners on third-base side, Padres on first-base side
- **Practice Times**: 9:30 a.m. for both teams
- **Gates Open**: Visitor infield, 12:10-12:25 p.m.; home infield, 12:25-12:40 p.m.
- **Ticket Line**: 800/677-1227, 623/773-8720
- **Ballpark Address**: 16101 N. 83rd Av., Peoria, AZ 85382
- **Directions**: From I-10: Take Loop 101 North. Exit Bell Road (exit 14) and head east. Turn south on 83rd Avenue. Peoria Sports Complex is approximately one-

quarter mile down on the east side of 83rd Avenue. From I-17: Take Loop 101 West and exit on Bell Road east (exit 14). From Bell Road, turn south on 83rd Avenue. Peoria Sports Complex is approximately one-quarter mile down on the east side of 83rd Avenue. There is plenty of signage.

Party Time in Peoria

Peoria Stadium is considered by many to be among the best ball-parks in the Cactus League, a status only enhanced with ballpark improvements unveiled in the past few years. The Seattle Mariners and the San Diego Padres share the ballpark, so a visit to Peoria, a suburb of Phoenix, during any point in spring training will undoubtedly find a game going on, with tickets available for most dates.

In the past, we were not very big fans of Peoria Stadium: it was not a comfortable place to see a game, with cramped concourses, a huge threat of substroke, and traffic jams galore. But the 2015 ren-

ovation designed by Populous addressed those issues, expanding
the ballpark footprint while allowing Peoria to overhaul concessions. That expansion also included a new, larger team store. All
in all, the improvements were well-chosen and increased capacity
while at the same time dispersing traffic throughout the ballpark.
Add in the general passion shown by Padres and Mariners fans for
both their teams and spring training, and you have one of the more
exciting atmospheres the Cactus League.

The Peoria Stadium footprint is now circular, with seating down
the lines brought in and reoriented toward the infield, as opposed
to the former orientation toward center field. There is a huge outfield berm seating 3,000, and it's packed most games. (Arrive
early to claim a good spot: the best spots in the outfield go
quickly.) All in all, the ballpark is very accessible, has good sight
lines, and can accommodate larger crowds very nicely.

Peoria Sports Complex was the very first MLB spring-training
facility shared by two teams. There had previously been many situations where two teams played games in the same ballpark but
maintained separate training facilities. Today, almost every new
training camp in the Cactus League is built for two teams.

The first round of improvements to Peoria Stadium came in February 2014, when the city unveiled a 56,224-square-foot clubhouse
for the Mariners and a 60,834-square-foot Padres clubhouse, complete with hydrotherapy rooms, dining facilities, administrative
offices, indoor and outdoor batting tunnels, and shaded patios. The
extensive facility allows both teams and their minor-league squads
to practice simultaneously. All in all, there are 12 MLB-sized
practice fields (two lighted), and four half fields.

Besides the expansion of the concourses and a new team store, the
biggest change to Peoria Stadium 2015 was the addition of a large,
shaded Group Pavilion Bar. This bar, featuring a large selection of
microbrews, macrobrews, and mixed drinks, is a welcome respite

for the sun-drenched fan, with drink rails, bar stools, and four tops galore. In front of the shaded bar is a group area with a great view of the field; if no group has rented it, it's open to the public.

More than any other Cactus League facility, any spring-training game at Peoria Stadium feels like a real event. There's always a lot of traffic and excitement surrounding a game—both the Padres and the Mariners draw well during spring training—and the games sport a carnival-like atmosphere. There are some who decry the location of the ballpark (set, essentially, in the midst of a series of strip malls), but fans seem to love the wide variety of restaurants within walking distance of the park. The ballpark and the games also feel like they are part of the local community: you can expect to see many members of the Peoria Diamond Club—the "Red Shirts" at games—who raise funds for local charities.

There's virtually no difference to how a spring game is run here. No matter who's the home team—and the first week of the season it won't matter a lot, as every spring the Padres and Mariners face off against each other several times—you can always expect crammed seating, a berm area teeming with families and expatriates, and a busy concession concourse. The only difference may be in the fans' complexions. For some reason, San Diego residents always look tanner and healthier than their pasty Puget Sound compatriots.

If you can, definitely hit a Padres or Mariners game in Peoria: it is one of the essential experiences in Cactus League spring training.

Ballpark History

Peoria Stadium was built for the Seattle Mariners and San Diego Padres, first opening in 1994.

The Spring-Training Ballpark Experience

Concessions

The food selection at Peoria Stadium is amazingly varied. Yes, there's the normal selection of ballpark foods—hot dogs, hamburgers, nachos, pizza, pop, etc. The hot dogs come in plain, foot long, and loaded versions with interesting toppings like bacon and cheese. If your palate runs to the more refined, you can seek out more exotic offerings like noodle bowls, gyros, roasted corn, BBQ, sno cones, chicken tenders, Philly cheesesteaks, fish tacos, teriyaki chicken, and hand-dipped ice cream.

The craft-beer selection had always been good at Peoria Stadium, but it hit with a new high in 2015 and 2016. Each end of the grandstand features a microbrew stand tied to each team (the Seattle stand, for example, is the Belltown Brewpub). Red Hook and Stone IPA are available, as well as the unique imported German grapefruit beer from Schofferhofer (yes, it's quite good).

In the outfield concourse you'll find a Four Peaks craft beer tent, as well as a Red Hook brewery tent. Four Peaks is probably the leading microbrewery in the Phoenix area these days (we discuss them in our overview of Phoenix and Scottsdale, as well as in our look at Tempe Diablo Stadium). Finally, two bomber stands offer a variety of the big bottles for $9.50. Take your beers over to the drink rails on both sides of the scoreboard, and you'll have a perfect view of the action. Or wander the park and find another spot; in general, the renovations added more drink rails to the mix.

Concessions are divided up into two areas: behind the grandstand and in the outfield. Heading to the concessions behind the grandstand means you'll miss some of the action if you decide to closely peruse the offerings. The outfield concessions, while lesser in number, are pretty good, with fish tacos, Philly cheesesteaks, chicken tenders, and burgers available in several stands. An all-you-can-eat deck is located in the right-field corner. Good food was always the order of the day in Peoria Stadium, but the new offerings raised the bar by a considerable amount.

Autographs

Neither team takes batting practice in the ballpark, opting instead to warm up on practice fields closed to the public. That means players show up just before the game, entering the ballpark from the right-field corner. Your best bet is to arrive early to the ballpark and attract a player or two to the edge of the stands or to hang out in the right-field corner and snare a player leaving the game. Players enter and leave the ballpark from this area. Position yourself next to the wrought-iron fence and snare players as they leave the game; many will stop and sign.

The Padres tend to gather near Section 122 before a game; we've never been to a game where a few players didn't head over to sign autographs.

Parking

There is a sea of paid ($5) parking adjacent to the ballpark. However, if you want to save a few bucks and grab a meal, dine at one of the many surrounding restaurants first and then walk over to the game.

Where to Sit

You have a wide array of choices for seating at Peoria Stadium, as the ballpark features a wraparound concourse and a large berm. The berm is crammed on a typical day, so arrive early and stake out a claim.

In the grandstand, you have your choice of theater-style seats (all 100-level sections, Sections 200-214, and all club-level seats in

Sections 300-303) or unbacked bleachers (Sections 215-220). In general, we advise avoiding the bleachers: they're hot and uncomfortable.

INSIDER'S TIP
Section numbering starts behind home plate; odd-numbered sections are down the third-base line and even-numbered sections are down the first-base line.

INSIDER'S TIP
To sit near the Mariners dugout, shoot for Sections 105-113 (odd numbers). To sit near the Padres dugout, shoot for Section 106-114 (even numbers).

INSIDER'S TIP
There's not a lot of shade at Peoria Stadium. Your best bet for relief from the sun lies in the area around Section 208, closer to the back of the grandstand, or in the outfield enclosed area. Otherwise, you'll face lots of exposure to the sun—so bring plenty of sunscreen or buy some in the team store.

Selfie Spots

Interestingly, one of the best spots for a selfie at Peoria Stadium isn't readily apparent when you first walk into the ballpark. The back of the center-field scoreboard is used as a marketing tool, proclaiming Peoria Stadium to be the home of the Padres and Mariners. It makes the perfect backdrop for a selfie.

If You Go

Where to Stay

Staying in Peoria is problematic. On the one hand, there are many hotel rooms available within two miles of the ballpark (some are located in Peoria, others in Glendale). But tour operators, who combine a hotel room with game tickets, reserve many of those rooms months in advance. The rooms that are available typically go for $175 or more a night—which is a lot to pay for a room during spring training.

To be within walking distance of the ballpark and have an affordable room, you'll need to make a hotel reservation almost a year in advance or buy a package from a tour operator. Here are the places within a mile of the ballpark:

- La Quinta Inn & Suites Phoenix West Peoria, 16321 N. 83rd Av., Peoria; 623/487-1900; *laquinta.com*. This hotel is located directly next to the complex; you'll have

to deal with a lot of traffic, but you'll also have a
ridiculously short walk to a game. This is also the
official hotel for both teams, so rooms can be scarce for
much of spring training.

- Comfort Suites Peoria Sports Complex, 8473 W.
  Paradise Ln., Peoria; 623/334-3993; *comfortinn.com*.
  Again, we're talking ridiculously short walk.
- Residence Inn Phoenix Glendale, 8435 W. Paradise
  Lane, Peoria; 623/979-2074; *marriott.com*.
- Hampton Inn, 8408 W. Paradise Lane, Peoria; 623/
  486-9918; *hamptoninn.com*.
- Holiday Inn Express, 16771 N. 84th Av., Peoria; 623/
  853-1313; *holiday-inn.com*.
- SpringHill Suites Phoenix Glendale, 7810 W. Bell Rd.,
  Glendale; 623/878-6666; *marriott.com*.

An alternative, should you not want to stay in the midst of a suburban strip mall, is just to stay somewhere else in the Phoenix area
and drive to the ballpark. In the middle of the day, the freeways of
Phoenix are not packed, so getting to the ballpark is easy.

RV Resorts Near the Ballpark

There is an abundance of RV resorts in the general vicinity of the
complex and a short drive away from the ballpark. A few are
located in adjoining Sun City, and the remaining resorts close to
the ballpark are located south on Highway 60, which can be a traffic nightmare. (No, there's no resort within walking distance of the
ballpark.) In general, these resorts are geared toward snowbirds
and not necessarily for short-term stays, so do some homework
and call ahead before assuming there will be a spot for you.

What to Do Outside the Ballpark

There are some who decry the suburban nature of Peoria, and
indeed the area surrounding the ballpark does have a strong subur-

ban feel, as chain restaurants sit comfortably next to local establishments. There are many outstanding restaurants within walking distance of the park. Most are located across 83rd Avenue, a short walk from the ballpark. (Peoria is marketing this area as P83, which you may see in some marketing materials.) There's been quite a bit of turnover in the area in recent years, so your fave from five years ago may be out of business.

Recommended: Slick's Garage, billed as serving New Mexican Cuisine. That really means a mashup of styles, with the common theme Mexican spices and peppers served on a variety of dishes, ranging from burgers to enchiladas. We'd also recommend eating and drinking out on the patio. *Slick's Garage, 8350 W. Paradise Ln., Peoria; 623/476-7605; slicksgaragepeoria.com.*

Also recommended: Firebirds Wood Fired Grill. A mix of upscale food in a rustic environment, Firebirds draws big crowds, especially on the weekend, with steaks and cocktails the big draw. *Firebirds Wood Fired Grill, 16067 N. Arrowhead Fountains Center Dr., Peoria; 623/773-0500; phoenix-peoria.firebirdsrestaurants.com.*

You'll find a marriage of cultures at Headquarters Grill Bar Sushi: sushi meets pulled pork meets sports bar. Yes, that does translate into something for everyone. *Headquarters Grill Bar Sushi, 16041 N. Arrowhead Fountains Center Dr., Peoria; 623/547-5577; headquartersaz.com.*

Worth a visit: Abuelo's. Though it's a chain (there are Abuelo's in Texas, Oklahoma, Ohio, and beyond) and the décor is a little over the top, the food at Abuelo's is decent. Go for the cilantro lime soup as an appetizer and the stuffed chicken-breast medallions. It's also the perfect place to eat before the game, as you can dine and then leave your car there while you walk a block to the ballpark. *Abuelo's, 16092 Arrowhead Fountains Center Dr., Peoria; 623/878-8282; abuelos.com.*

You'll find some Padres fans before and after games at Oggi's Pizza & Brewing. (Of course, Oggi's is headquartered in southern California, so the link isn't that absurd.) Microbrewed beers and trendy designer pizzas are featured. *Oggi's, 6681 W. Beardsley Rd., Glendale; 623/566-8080; oggis.com.*

If you want something more mainstream, there are a number of chain restaurants close to the ballpark, including Famous Dave's, Cheesecake Factory, Texas Roadhouse, and MOD Pizza.

Worth the drive: Arrowhead Grill, a high-end steakhouse known for its 10-ounce Delmonico, lovingly slathered in lemon butter, and the 48-ounce porterhouse (really). Don't let the Glendale address fool you: it's less than two miles from Peoria Stadium. Drive north on 83rd Avenue and then hang a right on Union Hills Drive. *Arrowhead Grill, 8280 W. Union Hills Dr., Glendale; 623-566-2224; arrowheadgrill.com.*

Other than dining, drinking, shopping, and golf, there aren't too many other attractions in Peoria. One attraction perfect for the entire family is the Challenger Space Center, which features exhibits on the history of America's manned-space program from Project Mercury through the space shuttles. It also contains Arizona State's Center for Meteorite Studies. *Challenger Space Center, 21170 N. 83rd Av., Peoria; 623/322.2001; azchallenger.org.*

Spring-Training History: San Diego Padres

The San Diego Padres have trained in Arizona since their National League inception in 1969. The team trained in Yuma from 1969 to 1993, moving to the new ballpark in Peoria in 1994.

Spring-Training History: Seattle Mariners

The Seattle Mariners have trained in Arizona since their American

League inception in 1977. From 1977 to 1993, the team trained in Tempe. In 1994, the team moved to the new ballpark in Peoria.

SALT RIVER FIELDS AT TALKING STICK / ARIZONA DIAMONDBACKS / COLORADO ROCKIES

QUICK FACTS

- **Capacity**: 11,000
- **Year Opened**: 2011
- **Dimensions**: 345L, 390LC, 410C, 390R, 345R
- **Dugout Locations**: Diamondbacks on the third-base side, Rockies on the first-base side
- **Practice Times**: Gates open at 9 a.m.
- **Gates Open**: Two hours, 10 minutes before game time. Home batting practice, to 11:15 a.m.; visitors batting practice, 11:15 a.m.-12:15 p.m.; home infield,

12:15-12:25 p.m.; visitors infield, 12:25-12:35 p.m. Add
six hours for a night game.

- **Ticket Lines**: 888/490-0383 or 480/362-WINS (9467)
- **Address**: 7555 N. Pima Road, Scottsdale, AZ 85258
- **Directions**: From Loop 101 (Pima Freeway)
  northbound: Take exit 44 (Indian Bend Road) and turn
  left, proceeding west for approximately 0.6 miles. Turn
  right at N. Pima Road. The ballpark will be located on
  your right. From Loop 101 (Pima Freeway) southbound:
  Take exit 43 (Via De Ventura) and turn right,
  proceeding west for approximately 0.8 miles. Turn left
  at N. Pima Road. The ballpark will be located on your
  left.

State of the Art in Scottsdale

It's the only spring-training ballpark to be built on tribal land and
the most popular when it comes to attendance. It's also a great
place to take in a game, representing the state of the art in spring-

training facilities. Unless you're truly strapped for time or don't want to venture past a favorite facility, a visit to Salt River Fields at Talking Stick should be on the agenda for anyone visiting Phoenix for Cactus League action.

For decades, the approach to a spring-training facility was pretty static: there was a main ballpark where games were played, with a couple of open fields for practices, drills, and minor-league workouts. The widely accepted premise was, if it was good enough for Connie Mack at Fort Myers' Terry Park in 1925, it was good enough for every other MLB team.

But designers of more recent spring-training facilities have walked away from this model. The new goal for architects and team management is to integrate what fans love about spring training—player access, warmer weather, a relaxed atmosphere—with the daily functionality of the complex. The HKS Sports & Entertainment Group first addressed these issues with Camelback Ranch—Glendale, which opened in 2009, and reinvented them at Salt River Fields at Talking Stick.

That new approach is apparent when fans first approach the complex. Instead of herding fans to one or two ballpark entrances, Salt River Fields at Talking Stick gives them four different and distinct entrances. The ballpark is placed at the center of the complex, allowing fans to meander through practice fields before the game. Large angled roofs provide plenty of shade. The berm is the largest in spring training, providing space for 4,000 fans to do what they really love at spring training: grab a cold one and sprawl out in the sun. Want to just hang out? There are tons of spots on the concourse, especially beyond the bases, to just sit down and relax. With running water on the west side of the complex, the ballpark feels like an oasis, especially on a hot spring day. Add to that a strong presence from the Salt River Pima-Maricopa Indian Community (SRPMIC)—the project hosts—and you have a unique spring-training environment.

How strong? The history of the Maricopa and Pima tribes is displayed prominently on displays at the ballpark. Restroom signage is in three languages: Maricopa and Pima tribal languages as well as English.

There are some similarities between Camelback Ranch and Salt River Fields. Both place the ballpark in the center of spring action and surround it with training facilities. And both rely on lots of natural finishes and colors. But Salt River Fields takes the lessons and extends them further with some local touches. There's plenty of shade in and around the ballpark in the form of ramadas. And there's no blocky ballpark exterior wall; fences guide your way.

If it sounds like we recommend a visit to Salt River Fields at Talking Stick: we do, wholeheartedly. A trip to the Cactus League wouldn't be the same without a trip to a Diamondbacks or Rockies game.

INSIDER'S TIP
There are four entrances. Many fans will enter the ballpark from a main entrance behind home plate after crossing a bridge over a water feature, while other fans will enter at the center-field gate, nearest the most parking. (The water feature is also functional: recycling water for future use on the playing fields.) There are ticket offices at all four gates, as well as Will Call windows at all four gates. You don't need to circle the ballpark to find a Will Call window if you've ordered tickets online, but you will need the correct window if a friend or ticket service has dropped off ducats for you.

INSIDER'S TIP
Diamondbacks and Rockies home games start at 1:10 p.m. or 7:10 p.m.

The Spring-Training Ballpark Experience

Concessions

Most of the stands offer the ballpark basics: hot dogs (including seven variations at Home Plate Hot Dogs), burgers, pizza, ice cream, and more. A dedicated barbeque stand offers up pulled pork and a BBQ trio plate. The national headquarters for Cold Stone Creamery is to the north of the ballpark on Via de Ventura (alas, it's just a standard-issue office building, not a Wonka-esqe shrine to the fine art of ice-cream making), so there's the requisite Cold Stone ice cream available.

> **INSIDER'S TIP**
> The 400-capacity Pepsi Patio at the top of the grandstand has one big selling point: you'll have a great view of virtually every mountain of note surrounding the Valley of the Sun, including Red Mountain and the Four Peaks. It's the best party spot in the Cactus League, featuring bar stools, drink rails, high tops, and an abundance of flat-screen TVs, perfect for monitoring during March Madness—all for $20.

Worth seeking out: margaritas served at stands run by local vendors Salty Senorita and Blue Martini, as well as vodka lemonades and sangria at dedicated concourse stands. (In fact, there are some folks who head to the ballgame and spend most of their time watching the action from the right-field Salty Senorita stand seating.) It's hard to miss the $10 sangria stand and the dedicated Jack Daniels and Absolut stands on the main concourse. Also worth seeking out: lobster rolls from the Cousins Maine Lobster food truck.

The beer selection is OK: mixed in with MillerCoors pretend craft beers (Leinie, Blue Moon) are some legitimate craft beers, such as offerings from SanTan Brewing Company.

INSIDER'S TIP
No outside food is allowed in Salt River Fields at Talking
Stick. You can, however, bring in two sealed water bottles.

Autographs

Trails lead to the back practice fields from the ballpark. You'll
occasionally find some minor-leaguers working out on the way to
the ballpark. The practice fields have some interesting names. The
Diamondbacks fields, on the Desert part of the complex, are
named Devil's Claw, Jackrabbit, Mesquite, Quail, Ramada, and
Whirlwind. The Rockies fields, located on the Mountain side of
the complex, are dubbed Adobe, Cottonwood, Duststorm, Red
Clay, Red Mountain, and Wild Horse.

When in the ballpark, Diamondbacks and Rockies are encouraged
to sign autographs at the edge of the seating along Sections
101-104 (Rockies) and Sections 120-123 (Diamondbacks); they
usually start 40 minutes before the game and stay through the
National Anthem. On most days, players will sign in those same
locations after the game as well. This is a tradition, it seems; we
witnessed the same sort of behavior from D-Backs players when
the team trained in Tucson.

Unusual in this day and age: last spring the Diamondbacks scheduled a noon autograph session on the left-field concourse on most
game days.

Parking

Parking is plentiful in the four lots adjoining the ballpark; the site
can host 3,000 cars. The cost is reasonable: $5. The complex also
runs shuttles from one end of the parking lot to the ballpark if
there is a huge crowd.

For the Kids

A supervised wiffle-ball court opens an hour before the game. On Sundays, kids can run the bases after the game.

Where to Sit

There are 7,000 theater-style seats at Salt River Fields, while the berm has a capacity of 4,000—the largest in spring training.

Really, there's not a bad seat in the house. Sure, the seats down the line are farther from the action, but you have the advantage of sitting close to the bullpens and autograph areas. The sun is an issue down the third-base line, of course.

The ballpark orientation is askew from the traditional north-east baseline configuration to allow for more shade during an average 1:10 p.m. game time. This puts more seats in the shade: out of the 28 rows in the grandstand (16 in back of the main aisle, 12 in front), 85 percent of them will be shaded at some point in the game. In the back, you'll find an abundance of shade; the 12 rows in the front portion of the grandstand start in the sun and will be in the shade for the end of the game. And yes, there are sunscreen dispensers at the ballpark.

> **INSIDER'S TIP**
> Sections are numbered in a clockwise manner: Section 101 is the first section down the first-base line, while Section 123 is last section down the third-base line. While both sit far from the action, they each have an advantage: they sit next to the home bullpen.

> **INSIDER'S TIP**
> The Diamondbacks dugout is down the third-base line, and the Rockies dugout is down the first-base line. To sit near the D-Backs dugout, go for Sections 115-120; to sit near the Rockies dugout, go for Sections 104-109.

Selfie Spots

Logos are affixed to the team buildings past the outfield concourse, which makes for a nice backdrop. In addition, the team names are affixed to the exterior entryways for both teams; they, too, make nice backdrops.

If You Go

What to Do Outside the Ballpark

The Talking Stick Resort is across Highway 101 from the ballpark, providing gambling, Indian-casino style. (More on it in the next section.)

The Talking Stick brand extends to the Pavilions at Talking Stick, a shopping mall south of the ballpark. It's been revitalized in the last several years and now features some very good restaurants and quick-service establishments, ranging from Tia Shorty's and First Watch (for the breakfast set) to Chipotle and Starbucks.

You are only five miles away from downtown Scottsdale, which we covered in depth earlier in this book. To get there from the ballpark, go south on Pima to Indian Bend Road and turn right. Drive a mile west to Hayden Road, then turn left and drive for 2.5 miles until you reach downtown Scottsdale.

Where to Stay

The Talking Stick Resort is across Highway 101 from the ballpark. The 496-room/suite hotel features a 240,000-square-foot casino, two championship-level golf courses designed by Ben Crenshaw and Bill Coore, two pools with private cabanas, and several restaurants. (A nice evening would begin at the Wandering Horse Buffet and end up at the Players Sports Bar.) The Talking Stick Resort is part of the SRPMIC development efforts. This is by far the nicest accommodation close to the ballpark. *Talking Stick Resort, 9800 E. Indian Bend Road; Scottsdale; 480/850-7777; talkingstickresort.com.*

Speaking of the restaurants at Talking Stick: A good place to head after the game is the 15th-floor Orange Sky, which features even more spectacular views of the McDowells and Camelback Mountain. Sit on the patio and enjoy the view.

Across the street from the ballpark: Days Inn and Suites Scottsdale. The old Pima Inn & Suites has been remodeled with a new lobby and upgraded rooms. Normal room rates are around $125 a night; good luck getting a room for 2016. *Days Inn and Suites Scottsdale, 7330 N. Pima Rd.; Scottsdale; 480/948-3800; daysinnscottsdale.com.*

Within a short drive: the Hampton Inn & Suites Scottsdale-Riverwalk. Corporate all the way, but it's new and clean. *Hampton Inn & Suites Scottsdale-Riverwalk, 9550 E. Indian Bend Road, Scottsdale; 480/270-5393; hilton.com.*

Given your location, you could easily stay at almost any Scottsdale resort or downtown hotel.

> **INSIDER'S TIP**
> Given that most Diamondbacks live in the area, the team doesn't maintain an official spring hotel. The Rockies do: The Scottsdale Plaza Resort (*7200 N. Scottsdale Rd., Scottsdale; 480/948-5000; scottsdaleplaza.com*).

Spring-Training History: Arizona Diamondbacks

The Arizona Diamondbacks have trained in Tucson (1993-2010) and Scottsdale, Az. (2011-present).

Spring-Training History: Colorado Rockies

The Colorado Rockies have trained in Tucson (1993-2010) and Scottsdale, Az. (2011-present).

SCOTTSDALE STADIUM / SAN FRANCISCO GIANTS

QUICK FACTS

- **Capacity**: 12,000
- **Year Opened**: 1992
- **Dimensions**: 360L, 430C, 330R
- **Dugout Location**: First-base side
- **Practice Times**: Workouts begin at 9 a.m. The Giants usually practice at Scottsdale Stadium or an adjoining diamond.
- **Gates Open**: Gates open two hours before game time. Giants batting practice, 10-11 a.m.; visitors batting practice, 11:15 a.m.-12:15 p.m.; visitors infield, 12:15-12:30 p.m. Add six hours for an evening game.
- **Ticket Line**: 877/4SF-GTIX (877/473-4849)
- **Address**: 7408 E. Osborn Rd., Scottsdale, AZ 85251
- **Directions**: The ballpark is located at Osborn Road and North Drinkwater Boulevard (formerly Civic Center Drive), two blocks east of Scottsdale Road. There are

plenty of signs pointing the way. If you lose your way,
follow signs to two ballpark neighbors: the Scottsdale
Civic Center and Scottsdale Healthcare.

A Southwestern Atmosphere in Scottsdale

With a pleasant Southwestern design scheme and an efficient layout, Scottsdale Stadium is located in the middle of downtown
Scottsdale and is one of the hottest tickets in the Cactus League.
It's one of the best spring-training experiences in Arizona: you
should plan on devoting a full day to walking the streets of downtown Scottsdale and taking in a Giants game.

Scottsdale bills itself as being a true Wild West town. Located just
outside of Phoenix, Scottsdale has a totally different look and feel
than the rest of the Valley of the Sun. There's some genuine history in downtown Scottsdale, and over the years the area has
evolved from being a kitschy little outpost outside of Phoenix to
an affluent suburb. When you visit Scottsdale Stadium, be prepared to do some battle with BMW sedans and Audi convertibles
on the roadways.

The centerpiece in the spring is Scottsdale Stadium. Today's ballpark is a renovation of the original 1955 Scottsdale Stadium, the former Cactus League home of the Baltimore Orioles, Boston Red Sox, Chicago Cubs, and Oakland A's. Its renovation was overseen by Populous and it has all the retro decorative touches you'd expect from a Populous ballpark, including lots of wrought iron and brick facades. It features 8,500 fixed seats, with room for 2,000 on outfield berms.

But one other signature feature of a Populous ballpark doesn't get as much attention as the retro features: Populous's propensity for breaking down a ballpark into very discrete elements. This means that fans can view the action from many different and unique viewpoints, an approach that works very well at Scottsdale Stadium. Most fans will want to camp out in the grandstand seating, which is fairly shaded from the Arizona sun, but for those wanting a more casual viewpoint there's a larger picnic area down the third-base line, outfield berm seating, and a casual standing-room-only area down the first-base line. (Indeed, we love heading to the right-field corner and hanging out with the casual fans and the cacti. It just screams Arizona.) There really is not a bad seat in the house.

INSIDER'S TIP
The outfield berm is a great place to watch a game. Be prepared for a steep walk out there, though. Our favorite spot in the outfield is in center field; a beer guy patrols the area so you never have to leave.

The ballpark atmosphere is relatively subdued—instead of the loud rock music blaring before a game, you'll hear an organist.

Another great thing about Scottsdale Stadium is its location: on the edge of downtown Scottsdale. Your best bet is to arrive early to the game and park for free in a city-owned covered parking ramp directly north of the ballpark: your car will enjoy the respite from the hot Arizona sun, and you'll have a chance to walk the two blocks to downtown Scottsdale. Otherwise, there's usually plenty of street parking in the general vicinity. Downtown Scottsdale is very safe, so don't be afraid to leave your car in an area marked for longer-term parking.

INSIDER'S TIP
Scottsdale Stadium is also home to the Arizona Fall League Hall of Fame and the Scottsdale Sports Hall of Fame. The Arizona Fall League is where major-league teams send prospects after the regular season to play under elite conditions, and members of the AFL Hall of Fame include the likes of Todd Helton and Derek Jeter. The Scottsdale Sports Hall of Fame honors notable locals, including Jim Palmer.

Having said this, there are plenty of issues with Scottsdale Stadium. It seats 12,000, but a crowd of that size leads to cramped concourses, elbow-to-elbow seating on the berm, and long lines at the concessions. With that in mind, the City of Scottsdale is debating another overhaul of the ballpark and the minor-league camp. Among the potential Scottsdale Stadium upgrades: adding more shade to the grandstand seating with an expanded roof; upgraded clubhouses; upgrade of bleacher seating down each line to chair-back seats; more parking with an expansion of the Civic Center Parking Garage, perhaps with an upgraded walkway into the ballpark; and expanded press box. This won't happen any time soon: the planning study isn't set to be completed until July 2017.

The San Francisco Giants are a major draw for spring training. The local community supports the team, Giants fans still make the trek to Scottsdale, and the ballpark environment is the best in the Cactus League. When a traditional rival is in town—like the Oakland A's or the Chicago Cubs—the place is packed. Be sure to buy your tickets well in advance.

Workouts

The Giants practice at Scottsdale Stadium. Workouts start at 9
a.m. Most of the time the major-league squad can be found in the
ballpark; occasionally you'll see some specialized practices on an
adjoining full field and half-field.

Minor leaguers work out mornings at the expanded facilities:
Indian School Park, 4415 N. Hayden Rd. (at Camelback Road).
This is more than just a workout facility; it's a great newer complex designed to showcase players and provide comfort to fans as
they watch a practice. There's plenty of seating behind the main
practice field, and it's a pleasant walk south to see the more
remote workout fields.

To check on a practice schedule, call the complex at 480/
990-7972.

The Spring-Training Ballpark Experience

Concessions

Most of the concession stands are located behind the grandstand,
but that's not universally true. For instance, a brat and beer stand
is located in the left-field corner, affording you a view of the game
as you scarf down a grilled delight.

And, in general, the concessions at the ballpark are pretty well laid
out. Each section has its own limited concessions area (in other
words, you're never too far away from a beer or Salty Senorita
margarita vendor), so you should plan on grabbing your food
while en route to your seat. Or you can take a break from the
action and bring some good food down to the many picnic tables
located down the left-field line.

Among the more notable offerings: roasted sweet corn, Gordon

Biersch garlic fries, John Morrell hot dogs, Johnsonville brats, and fresh fruit (the strawberries and cream is a particularly nice delicacy). The beer is fairly expensive, but the selection is excellent: you can find Fat Tire, Anchor Steam, or Sam Adams on tap, as well as a huge assortment of bombers. If that's not strong enough for you, blended cocktails are also available.

Picnic tables are located in the left-field corner if you don't feel like bringing that burrito or burger back to your seat.

Autographs

The best time and place to score an autograph is before the game; Giants players are pretty good about coming over to the first row of seats and signing autographs (head for Section 129 when you arrive at the ballpark). Also, Giants players will stop in the walkway next to the dugout (leading to the clubhouse) near Section 118 and sign autographs before the game.

Parking

Arrive early to score a free parking spot at Civic Center Parking Garage, the covered parking ramp directly north of the ballpark, next to the public library on Drinkwater Boulevard. From there you can walk into the ballpark or walk a few blocks to Old Town Scottsdale. As a bonus, many of the entrepreneurs reselling tickets set up shop outside the parking ramp. The Giants are still a good draw, and most games come close to selling out.

Otherwise, there are many ramps and lots close to the ballpark, including the Parking Corral at East 2nd Street and Brown Avenue, but there's more than enough free street parking in the area as well if you're prepared to walk. We've never had issues parking in downtown Scottsdale on a game day.

INSIDER'S TIP

You don't need to park near the ballpark; you can catch the
free Giants Shuttle to the ballpark. The shuttle runs between
the Fifth Avenue Shops and Loloma Station Transit Station
(2nd Street between Goldwater and Scottsdale roads) and the
ballpark. It runs from 90 minutes before each game until 30
minutes after the end of the game; a new shuttle leaves every
10 minutes. For more information, call 480/312-7696.

Where to Sit

The outfield berm is a popular spot and is usually crammed for
every game. We're talking some serious numbers: it technically
holds almost 3,200 people. It also contains the Charro Lodge, an
all-inclusive seating area behind the Giants bullpen in right field.
It's not cheap, costing $90 to $150 depending on the opponent, but
it is a nice oasis in a very frenetic ballpark.

There are three levels of seating at the ballpark. In Sections
101-130 and Sections 200-216, you'll enjoy theater-style seating.
In Sections 300-316, you'll find bleachers with backs. In Section
A-H, you'll find bleachers with no backs. As there are more
bleachers than theater-style seats at Scottsdale Stadium—and the
chairbacks are largely taken up by season-ticket holders—chances
are good you'll be sitting on a bleacher.

INSIDER'S TIP
The seat numbering at Scottsdale Stadium puts Sections 101
and 102 directly behind home plate, with even-numbered
sections down the first-base line—next to the Giants
dugout—and odd-numbered sections down the third-base
line. To sit near the Giants dugout, go for an even-numbered
section between Section 106 and Section 118.

If you need or want shade, your choices are limited to 300-level
sections, between Section 300 and Section 310. At the beginning

of an afternoon game, only the back of those sections are in the shade.

INSIDER'S TIP
You'll need to stay alert at Scottsdale Stadium when sitting in the grandstand. The screen does not extend over the top of the seating, so a foul ball quite often lands in the seats.

If You Go

Where to Stay

Scottsdale is a great hotel town. In recent years the chain offerings have been upgraded to the boutique-hotel class. Add the resorts outside of downtown, and you have a great assortment of lodging options to choose from.

Your first call should be to the Hotel Valley Ho, an impressively retro facility that has been linked to spring training for decades. This was the spring base for the Chicago Cubs when that team trained in Scottsdale in the 1960s, and it's still a favorite base for Cubbies fans on spring break. The hotel opened in 1956 and still retains a lot of that Eisenhower-era ambiance, though it's been modernized since; turquoise remains the color of choice in many rooms. Go for the retro feel, stay for the pool and spa, and have a nightcap (or breakfast) at the ZuZu Lounge. It's not exactly close to the ballpark, so plan on driving. (Alas, another former Cubbie hangout in Scottsdale is now gone: the frumpy Hampton Inn is now Hotel Indigo, another boutique hotel with attitude.) *Hotel Valley Ho, 6850 E. Main St., Scottsdale; 866-882-4484; hotelvalleyho.com.*

In past year the official team hotel was the Hilton Garden Inn Scottsdale Old Town (*7324 E. Indian School Rd., Scottsdale; 480/481-0400; hilton.com*); it's still a solid choice for spring-training fans.

Five hotels are within a half-mile of the ballpark, giving you the chance to set up camp and walk to the ballpark every day. Comfort Suites is typical of that budget chain; just be prepared to pay a premium if you can get a room. *Comfort Suites, 3275 N. Drinkwater Blvd., Scottsdale; 480/946-1111; choicehotels.com.*

The Courtyard by Marriott belies that chain's reputation as a mid-priced location and charges more than $200 nightly during spring training, if you can snare a room. *Courtyard by Marriott Scottsdale Old Town, 3311 N. Scottsdale Rd., Scottsdale; 480/429-7785; marriott.com.* Similarly corporate and similarly situated: the Holiday Inn Express and Suites. It's popular, clean, and easily accessible—what more do you need? *Holiday Inn Express, 3131 N. Scottsdale Rd., Scottsdale; 877/863-4780; holiday-inn.com.*

A more upscale offering is the Saguaro Hotel, located north of the ballpark on Indian School Road. The Saguaro chain is as boutique as it gets; if you can't take a dose of attitude with your room (like a work desk adorned with a framed portrait of Roy Rogers), you probably should pass. But with every room sporting a balcony and a restaurant, Distrito Scottsdale, with a patio overlooking Civic Center Mall, the Saguaro Hotel just screams retro Scottsdale. Bonus: use one of the hotel bicycles to pedal to the game. *The Saguaro, 4000 N. Drinkwater, Scottsdale; 877/808-2440; the-saguaro.com.*

A good choice for families is Extended Stay America, which features kitchenettes and multi-bedroom accommodations. *Extended Stay America, 3560 N. Marshall Way, Scottsdale; 480/994-0297; extendedstayamerica.com.*

There's a large assortment of lodging in the greater Scottsdale area, so you should not feel compelled to stay in downtown Scottsdale. Resorts in Scottsdale are among the best in the world. We like two in particular:

- The Camelback Inn is a flagship resort for the Marriott

chain, featuring over 450 casitas (essentially, guest houses) with private patios. Before or after the game you can sun yourself beside one of the three pools. It's not cheap—try getting a room under $500 per night—but it does sell out. *Camelback Inn, 5402 E. Lincoln Dr., Scottsdale; 800/242-2635; camelbackinn.com.*

- The Phoenician is a pure luxury resort featuring a 27-hole championship course. You're paying for the privilege of being away from the madding crowds, but you're paying for a truly upscale experience with renovated rooms. *The Phoenician, 6000 E. Camelback Rd., Scottsdale; 800/888-8234; thephoenician.com.*

RV Resorts Near the Ballpark

The Scottsdale Trailer Corral is about a half-mile from the ballpark, a very easy walk on any given day. *Scottsdale Trailer Corral, 3202 N. Scottsdale Rd., Scottsdale; 602/947-8532.*

(480)947-8532

What to Do Outside the Ballpark

The ballpark is directly adjacent to the Marshall Way Arts District, which includes the Scottsdale Civic Center, the Scottsdale Center for the Arts, and the Scottsdale Museum of Contemporary Art. The mall between these buildings is a nice calm spot and well worth a stroll before the game. Right off the mall is a slew of restaurants and watering holes.

Otherwise, we cover the charms of the area in our Phoenix overview and its section on Scottsdale.

Spring-Training History: San Francisco Giants

The San Francisco Giants' franchise has held spring training in the following locations: New York City (1901-1902); Savannah, Ga. (1903-1905); Memphis (1906); Los Angeles (1907, 1932-1933);

Marlin, Tx. (1908-1918); Gainesville, Fla. (1919); San Antonio
(1920-1923, 1929-1931); Sarasota (1924-1927); Augusta, Ga.
(1928); Miami Beach (1934-1935); Pensacola, Fla. (1936);
Havana (1937); Baton Rouge (1938-1939); Winter Haven (1940);
Miami (1941-1942, 1946); Lakewood, N.J. (1943-1945); Phoenix
(1947-1950, 1952-1980); St. Petersburg (1951); and Scottsdale
(1981-present).

A Peek to the Past: Casa Grande

Worth a drive on an off-day: a drive down I-10 to Casa Grande to
see the former spring-training home of the Giants. Francisco Casa
Grande is still around and retains many of the unique touches that
made it such a charming spot for spring training.

Be warned: It still feels like the middle of nowhere, so imagine
how remote Francisco Casa Grande must have felt in 1962 when
the San Francisco Giants launched spring training at the spanking-
new $2-million resort. Located outside of small Casa Grande, the
resort was designed to be a total self-contained environment for
the Giants, featuring its own airstrip, 18-hole championship golf
course, pool, and multi-field complex. Next to it: a 3,000-seat ballpark used occasionally for exhibition games, although the Giants
frequently traveled to Phoenix for the vast majority of their games.

For Giants owner Horace Stoneham, the hotel and training complex was an investment in Casa Grande's future: it was to serve as
the training camp for the Giants in February and March, and a luxury resort the rest of the year. It was also highly speculative:
Stoneham hoped (and probably assumed) the new interstate highway would be located near town, making his resort a short hop
from the freeway. Alas, Interstate 10 was built far outside town to
the east, consigning Casa Grande to a future with limited growth
(a 2013 estimate put the population at 50,111). Stoneham's dream
of a prosperous resort never came true, and by 1980 the Giants
shifted spring-training operations totally to Phoenix.

Today the resort still remains a pleasant diversion should you need a break as you drive between Phoenix and Tucson: it's 50 miles south of Phoenix and 70 miles north of Tucson. It was renovated in 2004—to the tune of $8 million—and it still retains some of the charming baseball touches in the original design. The pool is shaped like a baseball bat, while the parking lot is laid out like a catcher's mitt. (Go up to the rooftop for the best view.) Within the resort are pictures from the days when the Giants trained there. Despite the renovation, the resort still has an early-1960s feel, and you'll want to spend a little time wandering the lobby and the grounds.

Gone are the practice fields and the ballpark, though the watching stand at the center of the practice fields still stands; you can imagine Alvin Dark or Herman Franks hanging out and measuring the spring progress of Willie Mays, Juan Marichal, and Gaylord Perry.

SLOAN PARK / CHICAGO CUBS

QUICK FACTS

- **Capacity**: 15,000 (9,200 fixed seats, 4,200 outfield-berm capacity, 1,600 suite-level seating)
- **Year Opened**: 2014
- **Dimensions**: 360L, 366LC, 410C, 398RC, 360R
- **Dugout Location**: First-base side
- **Practice Times**: Practices begin at 9 a.m.
- **Gates Open**: Grandstand opens two hours before game time; berm will stay closed if Cubs batting practice runs long. Cubs batting practice (at next-door administrative facility), 10:10-10:55 a.m.; visitors batting practice, 11 a.m.-noon; Cubs infield, 12:05-12:15 p.m.; visitors infield, 12:15-12:30 p.m.
- **Ticket Line**: 800/THE-CUBS.
- **Address**: 2330 W. Rio Salado Parkway, Mesa, AZ 85201.
- **Directions**: The ballpark is southeast of the Hwy. 202 (the Red Mountain Freeway, running east/west) and Hwy 101 (the Pima Freeway, running north-south) interchange. From Phoenix and points west: Take Hwy. 202 and head east. Take exit 8 (McClintock Dr.) and go

south. Go left (east) on E. Rio Salado Parkway and drive 1.3 miles. The complex will be on your left. From Scottsdale and points north: Take Hwy. 101 south to Exit 52. Turn left (east) on E. Rio Salado Pkwy. The complex will be on your left. From Tempe: Take E. Rio Salado Pkwy. (which runs north of downtown and ASU) three miles; the complex is on your left.

Wrigleyville in the Desert

The opening of Sloan Park was one of the biggest events in spring training 2014, as a sellout crowd was on hand to witness the start of the next era in Chicago Cubs spring training. In fact, the crowd of 14,486 was the largest ever in the Cactus League.

It was a record that would not last, as the Cubs drew larger crowds and ended up being a huge success in the new Mesa ballpark. It was just yet another interesting occasion in the long history of the Chicago Cubs.

In fact, the Cubs have had one of the most diverse spring-training histories of any MLB team, with bases ranging from Avalon Park on Catalina Island (Cal.) to Long Beach to Mississippi to Tampa to Scottsdale and Mesa. Former Cubs owner William Wrigley wasn't shy about leveraging the Cubs against his other real-estate investments, and so over the years baseball needs were secondary to promotional and personal needs. (We'll discuss some of them later in this chapter.) In recent years team ownership has settled for basic facilities like Rendezvous Park, Fitch Park, and Hohokam Park for training and games.

So it had been a long time since the Cubs had opened a new spring facility capable of generating a lot of enthusiasm from fans. That changed with Sloan Park, which has allowed the Cubs to set spring-training attendance records in both 2015 and 2016.

INSIDER'S TIP
The ballpark opened as Cubs Park. In January 2015 the Cubs sold naming rights and a Wrigley Field sponsorship to Sloan Valve Company, resulting in the new moniker.

Sloan Park is located in Mesa, but this isn't the same part of Mesa as Hohokam Stadium, spring home of the Oakland Athletics and the former Cubs spring home: it's part of a larger park area right on the edge of Tempe. It's not the most scenic of sites, with a water-treatment facility and a freeway serving as a grandstand backdrop. (Fans down the first-base line do have a decent view of the Superstition Mountains, however.) It's also not one of the most accessible locations, either, with just one four-lane road—Rio Salado Parkway—providing east-west access. (In other words, plan ahead and be prepared to wait in line for a parking spot before the game or to leave the ballpark after the game.) Streets do encircle the ballpark—Clark on the west, Sheffield on the east—and fans will probably drive around the ballpark to view workouts and check out the facility on a non-game day.

INSIDER'S TIP
Speaking of parking: We advise approaching the ballpark

from the east, past Riverside Park. (Feel free to come early: the park has also been renovated as part of the ballpark development and features climbing wall and towers of various heights, a splash pad, and a lake stocked with fish. This area is also home to a new Sheraton hotel.) General parking is to the east of the ballpark, while reserved/handicapped parking (the so-called red parking because of the red stripes placed on reserved and media slips) is to the west and south of the ballpark. Yes, there will be lines, and yes, there will be a wait.

A Cubs spring game has always been a mix of diehard fans (probably more than the average spring match) and those attracted to a more casual experience, hanging out on the berm with the likes of Ronny Woo Woo and downing an adult beverage or three. Still, Hohokam Park wasn't the friendliest of venues—you were pretty much assured of bad sunburn and a break from the game during a concessions run—and, worst of all where the Cubs were concerned, featured separate major-league and minor-league training facilities.

The new spring-training facility is in two parts, albeit in the same block: the ballpark is separate from a 65,000-square-foot administrative facility with 10,000 square feet of workout space, multiple clubhouses, team offices, rehab facilities, meeting spots and more. The workout space is spacious, with the latest in workout gear on two levels and plenty of Cubs branding within, including championship banners, logos on the actual workout machines, and a huge mural of Wrigley Field at one end. The workout area opens up via garage doors to a football field (yes, football fields are big in training facilities) and a shaded space. Multiple practice fields are to the west and east of the building. If you're going to watch a practice, this is where you'll go: the main training field is open to the public on one side, with some limited seating on hand.

The team dresses in this administrative space and then walks to the ballpark via a dedicated roped-off area before the game. It's not too daunting a barrier, and spring-training fans have plenty of opportunities to snare a player or 10 for an autograph before the game.

INSIDER'S TIP

You can enter the ballpark from any gate no matter your seat location, and there are three on the south side of the ballpark. Before the game, take a minute to walk along the south side of Sloan Park (the side facing Rio Salado Parkway) and check out the montage of Cubs logos and other retro Cubs touches on the ballpark exterior. The Cubs have always been the best-branded team in baseball, and a look at the changes in the Cubs logos over the years is a nice reminder of that branding.

Once in the ballpark, fans will be treated to lots of shade, plenty of (but too many) Wrigley Field touches, and upgraded concessions and amenities.

The Wrigley touches are there, but not overwhelming. The same type of bricks used in Wrigley Field have been installed in the backdrop as well as on the suite level. The lighting supports on the grandstand mimic those used at Wrigley Field, and there's plenty of steel on the second level to remind folks of the Friendly Confines. A clock atop the videoboard is the same design as the center-field scoreboard clock at Wrigley. The outfield dimensions are exactly the same as Wrigley Field. The pitch of the berm resembles the fabled Wrigley Field bleachers. And don't miss the baseball cards and evolution of Cubs logos painted on the exterior of the ballpark on the first-base side. Most fans will be parking east of the ballpark, and the natural tendency will be to enter the ballpark in the right-field corner, but walk around the exterior of the park past the first-base gates and enter the home-plate entrance to see the exterior touches.

The biggest fan attraction with a direct tie to Wrigley Field: a replica of the famous marquee installed at ground level down the right-field line. (Renderings of the ballpark showed this mounted on an exterior wall a la Wrigley Field and raised on a tower; putting the marquee on ground level was sheer genius.) Fans can request a custom message on the marquee and take a picture with their names displayed to the crowd. Yes, there will be lines of fans wanting to send a marquee photo home—but it's well worth the wait.

One more tie to Wrigley Field: bleachers in the outfield. The berm, which seats some 4,000, was designed with the same incline as the famous Wrigley Field bleachers, to emulate the Friendly Confines feel. Past that is a left-field structure, with concessions and restrooms on the ground level and seating on the top. It's quite a distance between the action and the EIGHTEEN | 76 seats, but the Cubs enhanced the rooftop experience with four sections of seating—two sets of bleachers, two sets of covered four tops—and plenty of concession stands. (Why 1876? It's generally regarded as the first year of play for the Cubs as a charter member of the National League, and it's also the year sponsor Budweiser debuted as a national brand.) You need a special EIGHTEEN | 76 ticket to be up in this area ($14 in 2015, depending on the opponent), but once you're there you'll find plenty of room at the four tops. (Warning: it's a sun field out there, and it got pretty toasty on the bleachers. Be sure to use some of the free sunscreen, located in dispensers near the restrooms.) The whole point is to mimic the Wrigley Field rooftop experience.

INSIDER'S TIP
If you want to be near the bullpens, head for the berms. Both are located on field level beyond the home-run fence, with the Cubs in left field and the visitors in right field.

Finally, we have the seating bowl and grandstand. The second level features suites and two 400-capacity event spaces at each end. Most fans will be assigned to one of the 9,000 seats within the 15,000-capacity ballpark, but expect the concourses to be crowded: lots of drink rails ensures plenty of fans will be hanging out in the back of the grandstand, watching the game with shade and a cool breeze coming in from behind home plate. (The grandstand was obviously designed to allow in as much breeze as possible. It does.) The Cubs and ballpark architect Populous designed the ballpark to feature plenty of shade in the grandstand: they estimate 60 percent of the seating is shaded at the beginning of the game, thanks to canopies over every section of grandstand, including two freestanding seating areas with their own canopies down the first-base line, with that number increasing to 70 percent by 2 p.m. For the 1:05 p.m. game time on Opening Day, that estimate would appear to be correct: by 12:30 p.m., all seats between the dugouts were in the shade, save the first four rows behind the home dugout. Sections 103-104 were partially in the sun as well. You'll also be in the shade at the concession areas behind home plate.

But you do pay a price if you sit in the most shaded seats: the last four rows down the third-base line have serious limitations. Overhang means you won't see the scoreboard, the only source of the game score/balls/strikes/outs in the seating bowl. In addition, the sound is extremely muddy under the overhang, as speakers are hung to provide clear sound toward those close to the field. Even though this is spring training, fans do keep score and want to hear the substitutions and other game information.

Does Sloan Park work? Yes. It's a vast improvement over Hohokam Park in every way: more shade, better concessions, better places to just hang out, and a enhanced, more fun atmosphere. It's in a better part of town as well, making a day trip to a Cubs game mandatory for anyone visiting the Valley of the Sun for spring-training action. The one thing from Wrigley that couldn't be replicated in the new ballpark? No ivy on the outfield wall.

The Spring-Training Ballpark Experience

Concessions

Come hungry. Try the Sheffield Dog: two hot dogs topped with bacon, cheese, fried jalapeno caps, onions, and diced green chilies, all wrapped in a flour tortilla. It's spicy, but not too spicy. Other items worth checking out: the Northsider Pastrami Burger (a half-pound burger topped with pastrami on a pretzel bun), the Windy City Garlic Steak Sandwich (exactly what the name says: a steak beef sandwich marinated in garlic and served with pepper), and a fresh fajita bowl. These delicacies aren't found at every concession stand, so you may need to take a walk between innings to find them. The main concession stands are located behind the seating bowl. (Tip: great food and shorter lines can be found in the left-field burger bar and center-field concessions.) Also worth seeking out: the ubiquitous Island Noodles stand and Portillo's Italian beef sandwiches.

And, of course, there's that traditional Cubs beer: Old Style. We can remember the days when Chicago wasn't a Bud town, but rather an Old Style town, and the fact the Cubs still serve Old Style is a nice acknowledgement of that past. Also worth a search at the Dos Gringos bar in the right-field concourse: Goose Island 312.

If Old Style or Goose Island isn't to your taste, there are plenty of domestic macrobrews (Budweiser, Michelob) and some mega imports (Corona, Dos Equis) at the World of Brews stand in left field.

There is food at the ballpark beyond the concessions stands as well. A dedicated food-truck area past right field features space for the popular food trucks, some shade, and picnic tables: it's fenced off so you don't need to leave the park to grab a bite. A kids' play area is adjacent, and because both areas are just beyond the concourse, parents can see the action while letting the kids play wiffle ball. An open square bar closes out the right-field offerings.

INSIDER'S TIP
Worth a visit to the food-truck area: the Iowa breaded pork tenderloins.

Autographs

There is no Cubs clubhouse in the ballpark; instead, the team dresses in the adjoining administrative facility and walks over on a sidewalk connecting to the ballpark. Their entrance to the ballpark is an administrative/media entrance to the left of the home-plate gate. That sidewalk is roped off, but fans are encouraged to gather there before the game to snare autographs before the game.

INSIDER'S TIP
There are six practice fields surrounding the administrative building, but one is used for batting practice and main team practices: the field to the east of the building, and the one closest to fan parking and access. The Cubs take batting practice on this field, which features limited seating in the form of bleacher seats and a small berm on the first-base side. In general, the major leaguers practice at this field and a second adjacent field.

The minor leaguers train at a cloverleaf of four fields—fields 3-6—to the west of the administrative building. There are bleachers at all four fields.

In general, Cubs players will head to the ballpark between noon and 12:30 p.m. on the designated walkway, sometimes riding in golf carts. Do not head into the ballpark when the gates open at 11 a.m. and expect to head back outside to snare an autograph: the official policy is that you're not allowed back into the ballpark if you leave. Now, we also found that policy isn't uniformly enforced, and we've seen ushers stamp the hands for those seeking to dash out for an autograph. (We attribute this to volunteers and staff still working out the procedures after the opening of a new ballpark.) But in general, if autographs are what you seek, do not enter the ballpark until you've had a chance to work the line.

Otherwise, head to the dugouts and bullpens before a game and attempt to flag down a player. There's nothing official at all about this approach, and it's largely hit and miss, subject to the whims of players at any given time.

Parking

There is plenty of parking at Sloan Park for $5 or $10 (depending on the day). In general, the parking areas to the south are reserved for those holding handicapped passes, season-ticket holders, and VIPs—the so-called red parking because of the red stripes placed on reserved and media slips. Most of you will end up parking in the unpaved area to the east of the ballpark.

There are four gates at Sloan Park: home plate, first base, right field, and center field. If you park in the east fields, the closest entrance will be right field. However, as we noted earlier in this chapter, take the time to walk around the south side of the ballpark and enjoy the mural of Cubs logos.

And many of you will need to head to the south side of the ballpark, as the ticket office is next to the right-field gate, where you'll pick up Will Call tickets. If you don't have tickets, you can buy them at booths at the right-field and center-field gates, or the automatic ticket kiosks at the right-field gate.

INSIDER'S TIP

Tempe runs a trolley service from downtown to Sloan Park. The pick-up and drop-off location is located at the northwest corner of Mill Avenue and 5th Street (directly in front of

Lotions & Potions). You can park for free at the City Hall
Garage (117 E. 5th St.) after having your ticket validated by
the trolley driver. The trolleys begin circulating two hours
prior to the start of home games, running every 20 minutes
between Mill Avenue and Sloan Park, concluding 30 minutes
after the end of each game.

Where to Sit

Most fans will have theater-style seats with cupholders. The ballpark design allows for 70 percent of the seating to be shaded for
most of the game.

Because of the extensive shade, you can be pretty flexible about
where you sit. The Cubs dugout is on the first-base side, so anything in sections 100-110 will give you a good view of the home
team.

INSIDER'S TIP
The "away" seating down the right-field line are bleachers.
Nice home-field advantage for Cubs fans.

Like most new ballparks, Sloan Park is designed to be a neighborhood of seating areas. The sections behind the Cubs dugout is one
neighborhood. The fans standing behind the stands next to first
base is another neighborhood. The fans bellying up to the drink
rails in the concourse is another neighborhood. The fans in the
berm and the EIGHTEEN | 76 section are in two other neighbor-
hoods. There are many ways to view the onfield action in the ballpark, so you'll never tire of Sloan Park.

Selfie Spot

Is there any doubt? In front of the Wrigley Field marquee, of
course. Also worth a look: the montage of Cubs logos on the exterior of Sloan Park.

If You Go

What to Do Outside the Ballpark

When you finally get a chance to leave Sloan Park in the post-game snarl, you'll have two choices for your next destination; To the east (left), past Riverside Park: Mesa Riverview and downtown Mesa. To the west (right): Tempe.

Mesa Riverview has a number of nice watering holes, but we're partial to The Brass Tap, which features more than 300 draft and bottled beers. There's live music on the weekend as well. The food is strictly pub grub—but, hey, you're on vacation. *The Brass Tap, 1033 N. Dobson Rd., Mesa; 480/610-2337; brasstapbeerbar.com.*

The ballpark is northwest of downtown Mesa; while other communities in the Valley of the Sun are forced to create downtowns from scratch, Mesa has a historic one. Downtown Mesa has its own historic districts and attractions; you could do worse than spending time driving around and taking in a show or exhibit at

the Mesa Arts Center (*1 E. Main St., Mesa; 480/644-6500;
mesaartscenter.com*). In general, Main Street east of Hwy. 87 is
where you'll find the better restaurants in the city: a mix of Mexican eateries, coffeeshops, and Diamond's Sports Grille, a decent
sports bar. Visit *downtownmesa.com* for more information. In
downtown you'll also find one of the Phoenix area's better brewpubs: Desert Eagle Brewing Company (*150 W. Main St., Mesa;
480/656-2662; deserteaglebrewery.com*).

Heading west of the ballpark is your best bet for a wide selection
of food and drink, as you're a short drive from the many offerings
of downtown Tempe and environs. We cover those offerings in
more depth in our Los Angeles Angels of Anaheim chapter. We do
have four special recommendations west of the ballpark.

Bar Louie at the Tempe Marketplace is an upscale pub so much in
vogue throughout the Valley. The food is good and isn't just your
average bar food, and the beer/wine/cocktail selection is quite
good as well. For a quiet, relaxing spot after a raucous day at the
ballpark. *Bar Louie's, 2000 Rio Salado Pkwy., Tempe;
480-658-1600; barlouie.com.*

It's a little off the beaten path in an area filled with low-slung
industrial buildings, but Spinato's serves some of the best pizza in
the Valley. The combination of sweet tomato sauce and an outstanding thin crust will please even the most hardcore deep-dish
fan cheering on his or her Cubbies. *Spinato's, 27 S. Smith Rd.,
Tempe; 480/967-0020; spinatospizza.com.*

Tempe Marketplace is to the west of the ballpark. Many of you
will pass it on the way to the game, as it's located right on West
Rio Salado Parkway, and pretty impossible to miss. There are a
slew of restaurants there for any level of fan or family, but
Chicago fans will want to check out Portillo's, which claims to sell
a pretty authentic and tasty Chicago-style dog and Italian beef
sandwich with sweet peppers. The claim is believable: it is a

Tempe outpost of the Chicago original. *Portillo's Hot Dogs, 65 S. McClintock Dr. (at Rio Salado Pkwy.), Tempe; 480/967-7988; portillos.com.*

Finally: Four Peaks Brewing Co., a brewpub and restaurant known for its patio, fresh beer (quaff a Hefeweizen if it's on tap), and good food. Expect a crowd, even if you're visiting during spring break. *Four Peaks Brewing Co., 1340 E. 8th St., Tempe; 480/303-9967; fourpeaks.com.*

Really, the move gives Cubs fans to create some new traditions, as everything is changing: Sluggo's is gone, Hohokam Stadium is now the home of the Oakland Athletics, and Theo Epstein and crew are working hard to remake the franchise. And there are worse places for Cubs fans to gather than Four Peaks, Portillo's, or Logan's Roundhouse.

Where to Stay

The Sheraton Mesa (*860 N. Riverview, Mesa; 480/664-1221; star-woodhotels.com*) is an anchor of Wrigleyville West, a development between Sloan Park and Riverview Park. With 180 guest rooms—including 51 junior suites and 8 VIP suites—it should be a coveted venue for Cubs fans in 2016 and beyond, as it's the only hotel within an easy walk of Sloan Park.

You can either choose to stay close to the complex in what appear to be some marginal hotels or just pick out a nice hotel in Tempe or farther abroad in Mesa and make it your base. There are several hotels within two miles of the complex (which, depending on your tolerance for the sun, may or may not make them walkable), such as a Rodeway Inn or a nicer Hyatt Place. Extending your area to three or four miles—which would put much of Tempe in your search—opens the door to a much wider selection of nicer and affordable hotels. We do know this: The official Cubs hotel in 2016 was the Hyatt Place Phoenix/Mesa (*1422 Bass Pro Dr.,*

Mesa; 480/969-8200; hyatt.com), less than two miles from Sloan
Park. As a plus, you'll be close to a Bass Pro Shops and the Mesa
Riverview retail development, complete with lots of big-box
retailers and the likes of Logan's Roundhouse, Famous Dave's,
and our favorite, the Brass Tap. *Mesa Riverview, 1061 N. Dobson
Rd., Mesa; mesariverview.com.*

We also suspect many Cubs old-timers will continue staying at the
Mesa Mezona Inn (*250 W. Main St., Mesa; 480/
834-9233; mesamezonahotel.com*). We'd highly recommend it;
it's a traditional hot spot during spring training.

RV Resorts Near the Ballpark

The ballpark is in the northwestern part of Mesa, putting it a
decent distance from the many RV parks in eastern Mesa and
Apache Junction.

And there are an abundance of them, to be sure. Mesa is known in
some circles as being the RV park center of the Phoenix area.
That's not necessarily a bad thing. There are at least 16 RV parks
in the greater Mesa area, and that's not counting those in Tempe,
Gilbert, Chandler, and Apache Junction. Check out the likes of
Tower Point (*cal-am.com*), Mesa Spirit (*rvonthego.com*), and
Good Life (*cal-am.com*), but be warned that in general the RV
resorts in Mesa are really snowbird camps.

Spring-Training History: Chicago Cubs

The Chicago Cubs have trained in a variety of locations: Selma,
Alabama (1900); Champaign, Illinois (1901-02, 1906); Los Ange-
les (1903-04, 1948-1949), Santa Monica (1905); New Orleans
(1907, 1911-1912); Vicksburg, Miss. (1908); Hot Springs, Ark.
(1909-1910); Tampa (1913-1916); Pasadena, Cal. (1917-1921);
Catalina Island, Cal. (1922-1942, 1946-1947, 1950-1951); French
Lick, Ind. (1943-1945); Mesa (1952-1965, 1979-present); Long
Beach, Cal. (1966); Scottsdale (1967-1978).

Why Avalon on Catalina Island? Catalina Island is located 20
miles off the California coast, near Los Angeles, and Cubs owner
William Wrigley Jr. bought a majority interest in the island in
1919. Wrigley then constructed a ballpark on the island to house
the Cubs in spring training: it was built to the same dimensions as
Wrigley Field. (The ballpark is long gone, but a clubhouse built by
Wrigley to house the Cubs exists as the Catalina Country Club.)
By 1951 the team had grown disenchanted with Catalina Island,
however, and spring training was shifted to Mesa after the Cubs

held a profitable series of games against the New York Yankees in
Arizona. At the time Mesa was not seen as an attractive area for
spring training, and in fact the Oakland Oaks of the Pacific Coast
League failed to draw at all when the team held spring training at
Mesa in 1952.

INSIDER'S TIP

Interestingly, William Wrigley Jr. also owned the Arizona
Biltmore, which we discussed in our Phoenix and Scottsdale
overview, but never attempted to link the Cubs with a
Phoenix or Scottsdale training camp. Perhaps he felt pro
baseball was not a good fit with the upscale hotel, or perhaps
he felt committed to Catalina Island.

The move to Mesa was promoted by Dwight Patterson, a Mesa
rancher and builder who worked to bring spring-training games to
the area. The Cubs were hesitant to move to Mesa with the New
York Giants training only 20 miles away in Phoenix, so Patterson
and a group of local businessmen formed the HoHoKams, who put
up a $22,000 guarantee if the Cubs moved to Mesa's Rendezvous
Park. (Fittingly, Patterson was the first "Chief Big Ho.") Today
the Mesa HoHoKams exist as a charity and still work as volunteers for games at Sloan Park (they're the ones wearing the straw
hats and burgundy shirts, working the gates and the stands). The
Oakland Athletics play spring-training games at Hohokam Stadium, and the field at Hohokam Stadium is named after Patterson.
Rendezvous Park seated 3,000 when the Cubs moved there in
1952 but was expanded soon afterwards.

After the Cubs moved spring training to southern California in
1966, Mesa did not host any spring training until 1969, when the
Oakland Athletics moved their training from Scottsdale. Charlie
O. Finley was dissatisfied with the training facilities in Scottsdale;
hence the move to Rendezvous Park. The A's were not a big draw
in Mesa, however, and in 1976 Rendezvous Park was torn down to
make way for Hohokam Park.

SURPRISE STADIUM / KANSAS CITY ROYALS / TEXAS RANGERS

QUICK FACTS

- **Capacity**: 10,714
- **Year Opened**: 2003
- **Dimensions**: 350L, 379LC, 400C, 379RC, 350R
- **Dugout Locations**: Royals on third-base side, Rangers on first-base side
- **Practice Times**: Both teams hit the fields at 10 a.m.
- **Gates Open**: 10 a.m. opening on game days for both teams. Visitor batting practice starts at 11 a.m. no matter what team is home. Both teams take batting practice on adjacent practice fields.
- **Ticket Line**: 800/745-3000
- **Surprise Stadium Ticket Office**: 623/222-2222

- **Address**: 15860 N. Bullard Av., Surprise, AZ 85374
- **Directions**: Surprise Stadium is located 1 1/2 miles west
  of the intersection of Bell Road and Grand Avenue (U.S.
  Route 60, Exit 11). Bullard Avenue is located off of Bell
  Road, 1 1/2 miles west of Grand Avenue, or 2 1/2 miles
  east of Loop 303. You will be tempted to take Grand
  Avenue out from the center of town. Don't. You'll run
  into a lot of stoplights and run-down areas. Stick to the
  four-lane roads.

Surprise, Surprise

When Surprise Stadium opened over a decade ago, it was in the
middle of nowhere: suburban Phoenix had barely sprawled out
that far northwest, and there was precious little within walking distance of what many considered to be one of the finer facilities in
spring training.

Today, 15 springs after the arrival of the Texas Rangers and
Kansas City Royals from the Grapefruit League, there's plenty in

the general vicinity of may be the perfect place to see a spring ballgame: the sightlines are gorgeous, the concourses are wide, and the ballpark design is striking.

Built expressly for the Rangers and the Royals, Surprise Stadium features two 37,000-square-foot clubhouses with team kitchens, weight and training facilities, and administrative offices. In addition, each team has a practice infield, a football field (which is all the rage in spring training, interestingly), and six full practice fields. This changed in spring training 2016, when the teams will be receiving larger and enhanced clubhouses.

And since opening in 2003, the Surprise Stadium complex has aged pretty well. Though there are complexes coming closer to the ideal spring-training situation (i.e., Salt River Fields), Surprise Stadium still works as a player-development center and as a place to catch a game.

With the full Phoenix sun out for most games, you'll want to carefully choose where you sit. Both teams draw well in spring training, so a little planning is in order. But it will be worth the while, as Surprise Stadium is one of the most pleasant venues in the Cactus League.

The ballpark features a main seating bowl, a second level with both seats and luxury boxes, outfield berm seating, and a concourse ringing the ballpark. The best seats in the house are on the second level and within the middle seven or so sections of the main seating bowl: these are the seats that are shaded for the majority of the game. The main level of seats extends all the way down each line. If the middle sections are sold out, you're better off sitting down the line as opposed to a section facing the outfield, as the seats farthest down the line are angled to give you a direct view of the ballpark. Unlike most spring-training venues, there are cupholders at each seat, so you don't need to worry about some clumsy rowmate knocking over your $10 PBR.

The design is modern and clean. It does have a little touch of the retro that's proven to be popular in major-league parks like Oriole Park at Camden Yards, but not so much to distract you from your spring-training experience.

Technically, you're attending a game at Billy Parker Field at Surprise Stadium. Billy Parker was a former major-leaguer who worked with youth baseball programs before his death in 2003. He played parts of three seasons with the California Angels and hit a game-winning homer in his first game. Alas, he never got to see a game in the ballpark he worked toward as a city activist.

> **INSIDER'S TIP**
> Volunteers are very important at Surprise Stadium. You can tell the 700 or so volunteers—the Surprise Sundancers—because they are wearing yellow shirts. They act as ushers and ticket takers. Be nice to them. They are there because of love of baseball and community, not because they feel the need to deal with drunken slobs trying to crash the shaded second level.

The Spring-Training Ballpark Experience

Concessions

There are concession stands along the concourse, with one big food court down the left-field line featuring Southwestern foods, burgers, ice cream, pork tenderloin sandwiches, BBQ, and more. The hot dogs are worth seeking out: they may be roller-grilled, but they're plump and flavorful. Also worth checking out: a mac 'n cheese and bratwurst bowl, a bacon mac 'n cheese hot dog, toasted turkey, and more. Many food items are sold in combos, like the $12.75 BBQ sandwich combo that includes fries, soda, and peanuts. In addition, there's a separate concession area in back of center field for those watching the game from the berm. It's a hardy spot to load up if you're entering the center-field gate.

INSIDER'S TIP
The best buy at the ballpark is the $30 Budweiser Home Run Party Deck, located behind the right-field berm. You'll first need to buy a ticket to the game (we recommend a berm ticket), but then you'll have access to food (including entrée and dessert) catered by a local restaurant, as well as a drink (beer, water, or soda) ticket. The ticket also gets you access to a chained-off seating area with four tops. And should you want another drink, you'll have access to a bar limited only to those holding tent tickets.

The beer selection is much improved over recent years. It doesn't take much work to find craft beers like Shiner Bock, Four Peaks, Goose Island, Barrio Brewing, and Sierra Nevada on tap to go along with macrobrews like Bud and Michelob. The beer is also expensive: over $10 for tall boys. (Yes, it does seem outrageous to spend $10.50 on a Pabst tall boy that costs $2 in your average gas station.) If you want a little more kick in your cup, there's a cocktail stand down each line. Bonus: all the seats have cupholders. And there are picnic tables down each line as well.

Autographs

The biggest flaw in Surprise Stadium is its lack of good autograph opportunities, as neither team takes the field until just before game time. Both take batting practice on adjacent and off-limits practice fields, although at times you'll see some Rangers taking batting practice on the enclosed cages across the concourse from the first-base area. Your best bet is to hit the ballpark well after the gates open and try to lure a player to the stands after they enter the field and are heading to the dugouts. Be warned that both teams enter the field from the outfield corners; they do not enter through the grandstand or dugouts. (Fans of visiting teams should note: visiting teams enter from an entrance between sections 101 and 102 and will occasionally stop to sign.) Other than that, the pickings are pretty slim before and during the game. After the game you'll

occasionally see players hanging around as they walk from their
dugouts to clubhouses.

Parking

Free! 'Nuff said. There's plenty of parking next to the ballpark,
and it's all free, free, free. If you arrive close to the start of the
game and the main parking areas are full, you may be diverted to
parking at the next-door aquatics area. You're still close to the
ballpark, and the price is still right: free. If you have a ticket, head
right to the marked third-base gate; if you do not, head to the ticket
office near center field and enter via that gate.

Worth noting: the Sundancers often run golf carts throughout the
parking area to help those who may need a little help getting to
their seats.

> **INSIDER'S TIP**
> When you enter the ballpark, take a minute to reflect for a
> moment when you cross Buck O'Neil Way, which runs
> between Surprise Stadium and the parking lot. Buck O'Neil
> was one of the true pioneers of baseball, a crucial bridge
> between the Negro Leagues and some great teams on the
> Kansas City Monarchs and MLB integration. O'Neil began
> his playing career in 1938 with the Monarchs, later serving
> as a player-coach. After integration, O'Neil became the first
> black MLB coach, working for the Chicago Cubs. He later
> scouted for the Royals and was a fixture at Kauffman Sta-
> dium. If you saw Ken Burns' landmark *Baseball* PBS docu-
> mentary, you saw the sparkling wit that made O'Neil such a
> beloved figure in the game.

Connectivity

In past years Surprise offered free municipal WiFi in the ballpark.

This is unusual, to say the least, so take advantage of free WiFi if offered in 2017.

Where to Sit

We recommend either sticking as close to the middle of the grandstand as you can afford or head to the berm. When you get down both lines—say, in Section 115 and beyond—you'll find your seats are oriented toward center field, making for an uncomfortable twist of the neck if you want to closely follow the infield action.

> ### INSIDER'S TIP
> The grandstand seating begins with Section 100 and is divided by even-numbered sections up the third-base line and odd-numbered sections up the first-base line. To sit near the Royals dugout, go for even-numbered sections between 105 and 113; to sit near the Rangers dugout, go for odd-numbered sections between 106 and 114.

There's one more reason to seek a seat as close to home plate as possible: comfort. There's an abundance of shade at Surprise Stadium: every Upper Dugout seat—Sections 201-206—is located under a roof in the upper portion of the ballpark. In addition, these sections provide the overhang that shades the rear rows in Sections 101-112. These seats are a premium, as every retiree in the area knows enough to buy season tickets there. If you can't snare an upper-level seat, you'll find more shade in the first-base section at the beginning of an afternoon game.

> ### INSIDER'S TIP
> If your team is in the NCAA basketball tourney and you want to follow the action at the ballpark, spring for the Home Run Party Tent in right-center field. You'll receive access to the all-you-can-eat buffet, a drink voucher, and access to TVs tuned to all the March Madness action. And if you don't

care about basketball, you'll still have access to a tent with
four tops and shade.

The berm is also a perfectly acceptable place to watch the game.
It's big—seating 3,600 or so—and has its own concession stand.
Bullpens are cut out of the berm down each line, so you can watch
players in action as they prep for a game appearance. Plus, as
there's a wraparound concourse surrounding the playing field, you
can wander the ballpark to your heart's content.

That wraparound concourse makes it easy for those physically
challenged to make their way to handicapped-accessible seating in
the back of sections 101, 102, 107-112, and 117-120. In addition,
there is handicapped seating behind each bullpen in the outfield.

Selfie Spot

As with most Cactus League ballparks, there are some outstand-
ingly scenic vistas outside the ballpark. To see the White Tank
Mountains from the ballpark—or to capture them in the background for a nice selfie—position yourself in the right-field berm.

If You Go

What to Do Outside the Ballpark

Surprise is on the far edge of the Phoenix metropolitan area, and it's still an area in transition: it's currently a mix of housing developments (the original Sun City development is due east, while new Sun City developments are within the city limits to the west) and big-box retailers. When Surprise Stadium opened, it was in the middle of nowhere. And while you can still see nowhere from the ballpark (just look past Sun City Grand to the west), there's a lot more of note within a short drive of the ballpark than there was a decade ago.

Several years ago chains dominated the restaurants close to the ballpark, but these days you can find something a little more unique and regional within a very close drive. Places we can recommend include Saigon Kitchen (*14071 W. Bell Rd., Surprise; 623/544-6400; saigonkitchenaz.com*), Rito's (*15643 N. Reems Rd., Surprise; 623/546-3835; ritosmexicanfood14st.com*), and Babbo

Italian Eatery (*15609 W. Bell Rd., Surprise; 623/825-1919; bab-boitalian.com*). In addition, there are several more chain restaurants at the corner of Bell Road and Highway 60 east of the park.

Sure to be rocking on St. Patrick's Day: The Irish Wolfhound Restaurant & Pub (*16811 North Litchfield Rd., Surprise; 623/214-1004; irishwolfhoundpub.com*). No, we can't explain the inexplicable popularity of Irish bars in the Valley of the Sun past the fact that many retirees like to include a beer and some camaraderie in their daily routines, but the Irish Wolfhound usually attracts a crowd after a game.

Worth a little farther drive is Macayo's Mexican Kitchen. The Macayo's Mexican Kitchen chain dates back to 1948 and goes past a standard menu of tacos and burritos with specialties like chicken poblano and grilled salmon. *Macayo's Mexican Kitchen, 6012 W. Bell Rd., Glendale; 602/298-8080; macayo.com*.

Where to Stay

As the area around the ballpark has grown, so have the hotel choices in the area. There are two hotels within walking distance (under a mile) of Surprise Stadium:

- Residence Inn Phoenix NW/Surprise (*16418 N. Bullard Av., Surprise; 866/599-6674; marriott.com*)
- Holiday Inn Express Surprise (*16540 N. Bullard Av, Surprise; 855/799-6861; ihg.com*)

On the plus side, both hotels feature suites, perfect for a family vacation. On the minus side, both hotels will run you $200 or more a night, and apart from the ballpark there's not a lot within walking distance of the hotels, save the municipal complex with the aquatic center and library. Also, be warned that because the Rangers put up some players and staffs at these two hotels, openings can be hard to corral.

INSIDER'S TIP
The Royals team hotel is the Wigwam Golf Resort & Spa
(*300 E. Wigwam Blvd., Litchfield Park, 623/935-3811; wig-
wamresort.com*), a 400-acre, 331-room complex with three
18-hole championship courses. The Rangers occupy two
hotels in the spring: the aforementioned Holiday Inn Express
and Residence Inn.

Because there are so many spring-training venues in Phoenix and
you're more than likely visiting more than one ballpark, chances
are pretty good that you don't necessarily need to be staying close
to the ballpark, unless all you want to do is order takeout pizza
evenings after the games. Phoenix is a relatively easy area to make
your way around, so don't feel like it's essential you stay close to
the park. There are an abundance of cheaper chain hotels in Surprise as well as nearby Peoria and Glendale.

Spring-Training History: Texas Rangers

When the "new" Washington Senators entered the American
League in 1961, they established a spring-training camp in Pompano Beach, Florida, and stayed there until 1986, when operations
were shifted to Port Charlotte, Florida. (That Pompano Beach ballpark lasted for several years before being torn down in 2008.) The
Rangers moved spring training from Florida to Surprise in 2003.
Meanwhile, the Port Charlotte ballpark was renovated and is now
the spring-training home of the Tampa Bay Rays, Charlotte Sports
Park.

Spring-Training History: Kansas City Royals

When the Kansas City Royals moved spring-training facilities to
Arizona in 2003, it was the first time the team had not trained in
Florida in team history. From 1969 through 1987, the team trained

in Terry Park in Fort Myers, moving in 1988 to the brand-new
Baseball City Stadium in central Florida.

Baseball City Stadium was the centerpiece of Boardwalk and
Baseball, a 135-acre combination amusement park and baseball
facility in Haines City. When the development opened, the
7,000-seat ballpark and the six-field training complex were considered state of the art.

The amusement park, alas, was not. Owned and managed by book
publisher Harcourt Brace Jovanovich, the former Circus World
didn't have the attractions to lure families from Orlando or Tampa.
When HBJ restructured debt in 1987, it also closed down Boardwalk and Baseball. Eventually the amusement park was torn down
and replaced with a residential development. The ballpark and
ballfields sunk into disrepair after the loss of the Royals and were
finally, mercifully, torn down to make way for commercial development.

Ironically, Terry Park remains popular with high-school and college teams in the spring. Baseball City Stadium, declared state of
the art when it opened, is now long gone.

TEMPE DIABLO STADIUM / LOS ANGELES ANGELS OF ANAHEIM

QUICK FACTS

- **Capacity**: 9,315
- **Year Opened**: 1969; renovated several times since
- **Dimensions**: 340L, 400LC, 420C, 400RC, 360R
- **Dugout Location**: First-base side
- **Practice Times**: Practice usually starts at 9:30 a.m.
- **Gates Open**: 90 minutes before gametime. Angels batting practice, 10:45-11:45 a.m. (on adjacent field); visitors batting practice, 11 a.m.-noon; Angels infield, noon-12:15 p.m.; visitors infield, 12:15-12:30 p.m.
- **Address**: 2200 W. Alameda Dr., Tempe, AZ 85282
- **Directions**: Take Broadway Street exit off I-10 (coming from either direction); travel west on Broadway to 48th

Street; turn left; Tempe Diablo Stadium is 1/2 mile on
the left. Enter ballpark parking area by turning left on
Alameda.

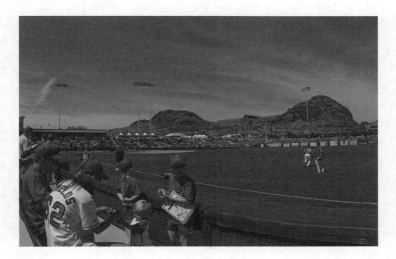

Devils and Angels in Tempe

The Cactus League is known for ballparks set in scenic locales, as
the many buttes and mountains ringing the Valley of the Sun provide wonderful backdrops to game action. Tempe Diablo Stadium,
spring home of the Los Angeles Angels of Anaheim, is the most
scenic ballpark in the Cactus League, bar none. With the Twin
Buttes beyond the left-field fence, a striking Spanish-style exterior, and a relatively remote office-park location that paradoxically
offers easy freeway access, Tempe Diablo Stadium is a gem, a
must-visit for anyone hitting Phoenix in February and March.

The ballpark itself is very fan-friendly. Renovations in 1993 made
the place a much more accessible venue, adding a concourse level
above the bowl housing a wide variety of concession offerings,
while a second set of renovations in 2006 expanded the training
facility and provided a new entrance. Throw in easy accessibility

to practice fields, located on the other side of the parking lot from the ballpark, and you have a great spring-training experience.

The two best things about the ballpark are its location and its layout. It's easy to get to—get on I-10 south, take the Broadway Street exit, and follow the signs—and there's plenty of cheap adjacent parking. Tempe is within 10 minutes of the Phoenix airport, which makes it easy to hop into the car and hit a game right after arrival. Phoenix is an easy drive from Los Angeles, which allows passionate Angels fans the chance to see their team in action at a great, intimate facility. A few years ago it was easy to snare an Angels spring-training ticket, but these days the Halos are one of the hottest spring-training tickets in the Cactus League. Plan ahead; the days of walking up and snaring a good ticket 30 minutes before game time are gone.

The original Diablo Stadium was built in 1968, but it was first expanded in 1993. The original playing field, seating bowl, and visitors' clubhouse were incorporated into the new facility, which added a new clubhouse, enclosed batting tunnels, and more.

In addition, the renovation added five concession stands, a concourse-level plaza area, an observation deck, and a picnic area down the third-base line. It's worth getting to the park early to snare one of these picnic tables, as they're fairly close to the action; however, their usability is somewhat limited by the fact that the Angels don't allow any outside food at all in the ballpark.

The latest round of renovations in 2006 added more training fields to the mix (six full fields in total), practice facilities and a minor-league clubhouse, as well as a new entrance to the ballpark. Previously the Angels had practiced at an offsite facility, but the latest expansion allows all the major- and minor-leaguers to train at the same location.

The layout of Tempe Diablo Stadium is standard, with most of the seating in the grandstand, roughly half armchair seats and half

bleachers. There is also lawn seating in left and center field. The
best seats are the box seats down the first-base line: you're definitely in a sun field, but the view of the buttes beyond the ballpark
is spectacular. There's a minimum of foul territory, so you're
never too far from the action—which includes rubbing elbows
with pitchers warming up in both bullpens down each line.

INSIDER'S TIP

Most new ballparks feature a below-grade playing field; it's
cheaper to dig down than build up. However, because the
ballpark is built on the side of a hill, the main entrance to
Tempe Diablo Stadium is at the top of a set of stairs. There
are handicapped-accessible ramps on both sides of the entry-
way.

There's a little bit of the retro at Tempe Diablo Stadium. The
scoreboard is old, the seating still features a slew of bleachers, and
the sightlines aren't great. But there's a lot of life at Tempe Diablo
Stadium: Angels fans fill the place up, families abound, and the
focus is on the game.

As if you can't tell, we adore a spring game at Tempe Diablo Stadium. It's not as spacious or luxurious as some of the new spring-
training temples, and you will have precious little chance to sprawl
out, either in your seat or on the concourse. But the Angels have
kicked up their level of fan commitment and the fans have
responded, making Tempe Diablo Stadium one of the great hot
spots in spring training.

The Spring-Training Ballpark Experience

Concessions

Food and drink were overhauled at Tempe Diablo Stadium in
2014, when Legends Hospitality—the concessions company co-
owned by the New York Yankees and Dallas Cowboys—took

over operations. As a result, some of the more unique offerings at Tempe Diablo Stadium went by the wayside, replaced by standard ballpark fare. Yes, it's all filling, and it's priced similarly to concessions at other ballparks. But to our subjective eye, it's not nearly as good as in past years, when the smell of mesquite grilling dominated the proceedings. (Don't worry: Diablo Dogs are still grilled the old-fashioned way.)

The place to find the best food in the ballpark: at the end of the left-field-line area, where local fare is represented by stands under the white tents. If you like Honey Bears BBQ (we discuss the local chain in other chapters; it's what passes for barbeque in Phoenix), you'll like the pork and beef tips found at a stand down the line. Similarly, you'll find Southwestern fare like tacos. If you do decide to eat at the ballpark, grab one of the four-tops or picnic tables in the area.

Most of the beer stands feature corporate beers, like Budweiser. Near Section 13 there's a stand with a wider variety of beers, including Fat Tire, Firestone, Four Peaks (which we discuss in more detail later), Coors, Deschutes, and Widmer. Expect to pay $11 for a good beer.

The Angels follow MLB rules when it comes to what you can bring into the ballpark. Water is $5 a bottle in the ballpark. Bring your own unsealed water and save a few bucks, or buy a few from one of the many vendors hawking water and peanuts outside the ballpark.

Autographs

There are six full and one half practice fields to the west of the ballpark, as well as a new clubhouse added when minor-league operations were moved to this facility. All are accessible to fans at the beginning of spring training, with the four main cloverleaf fields featuring covered seating. The two fields closest to the ball-

park, Fields 1 and 2, are reserved for the major leaguers. Practices
usually begin around 9:30 a.m.

When games start, get to the ballpark early enough to hang out in
the parking lot. Before the game, the Angels take batting practice
at the field directly next to the ballpark, then cut across the parking
lot while heading to the clubhouse. Batting practice is technically
closed off to fans, but you can line up along the left-field line and
view the action from there. The Angels cordon off a walkway for
players, but you can wait alongside it and snare some autographs.
Players usually walk from batting practice to the ballpark beginning at 11:15 a.m.

Inside the ballpark, plant yourself next to sections 21 and 22.
These sections are located next to the tunnel leading to the clubhouse, so players and coaches have no choice but to walk past fans
here. Also, players are known to hang around the visitors' bullpen
before games, so you should head down there and snag an autograph: it is located down the left-field line in foul territory. (The
home bullpen is located beyond the right-field fence, to the south
of the scoreboard: it's fenced off and not accessible to fans.) If
you're seeking the autograph of a visiting player, head down the
right-field line after the game and catch the attention of players
heading for the team bus. The parking lot to the east of the ballpark is secured, so you can't seek autographs next to the bus or the
right-field gate.

INSIDER'S TIP
The confines at Tempe Diablo Stadium are pretty tight, and
during batting practice—for the away team, as the Angels
take BP at an adjacent field—there are many balls flying out
of the ballpark. Most of what is hit past the home-run fence
in left field heads into the berm, but occasionally a ball will
leave the ballpark and end up on Westcourt Way, the street
running behind the ballpark and up to the Phoenix Marriott
Tempe at The Buttes. If you're a true ball hawk, head past

the right-field home-run fence in the parking lot and wait for homers there.

Parking

There are two main parking lots on the east and west sides of the ballpark, but in general the west lot is reserved for players, the front office, and VIPs. Unless you come to the ballpark really early, you'll be shuttled down to the east lot or other lots off Ajo Way. Some businesses also sell parking, but don't be gouged. Generally, the parking offered by the Angels is cheaper ($5). There is also limited street parking in the area, but be warned: the area is crawling with cops, and you will be towed if you're parked illegally.

Because the Angels have grown into a hot Cactus League ticket, it's in your best interest to arrive at the ballpark early. During our last visit we arrived at the ballpark an hour early and we still were presented with a huge traffic jam on Ajo Way.

You'll be directed to the front gate of the ballpark, in front of the steps behind home plate. If you park in the west lot, you'll walk right past the ticket office, located on the street level. (It's hard to miss.) Windows 1-6 are devoted to general sales; 7-8 are reserved for Will Call.

Where to Sit

Not every seat is created equal, as there are slightly more backed bleachers than chairback seats at Tempe Diablo Stadium, with the chairbacks, complete with cupholders, installed between the dugouts. Ducats to an Angels game aren't impossible to buy, but good seats are at a premium.

You'll want to sit in the last four rows of the grandstand (rows W and higher) behind home plate or on the first-base side if you pre-

fer to avoid the sun; a canopy covers concessions, not seats. (Try
the back of section 12 for a good, shaded seat.) There are 24 seating sections at Tempe Diablo Stadium, with Section 1 beginning
down the left-field line and ending with Section 24 down the right-
field line. To be close to the home dugout and potential eye con-
tact with Mike Trout, go for seats in sections 15-18. Speaking of
avoidance: don't sit in sections 23 or 24, as they're angled toward
center field, and your views of the infield will be blocked by fans
in adjoining sections. These sections are sold cheaply as Grandstand seating (a misnomer, as these seats aren't technically part of
the grandstand), but you're better off grabbing a four-top down the
left-field line or camping out on the berm. Better choices are section 22 and 21—which feature raised bleachers—while sections
1-4 and 18-20 feature bleacher seating as well.

Of course, if you want to avoid the sun altogether, you can spring
for a suite on the press-box level. There are two suites at the ballpark.

INSIDER'S TIP
Yes, that's Tempe Diablo Stadium on the cover of this book.
The view of the buttes comes from a vantage point on the
first-base side. A third-base seat yields a much more average
view of the freeway and the parking lot.

One underrated area of seating: the $10 berm, which runs down
the left-field line and wraps around the foul pole into left field,
seating 2,300 or so. As a bonus, the berm seating overlooks the
away bullpen, and there's generally a lot of room out there.

INSIDER'S TIP
Worth the cost: an inclusive buffet on the suite level down
the first-base line features a nice view of both the playing
field and the distant scenery.

With the ballpark featuring a raised concourse, handicapped seating can be found at the back of sections 2-7, 9, 13, and 15-22. The

Tempe Diablos have a reputation for being helpful and will run a golf cart out to transport folks who face mobility challenges.

For the Kids

Though we often note many families at the ballpark—and let's face it, the backed bleachers are great for families, no matter what some may say—there is not a lot at the ballpark geared specifically for kids. The steep berm may even pose some challenges for toddlers.

Selfie Spot

The best spot for a selfie is probably from your seat, with the buttes as a background.

If You Go

What to Do Outside the Ballpark

There's really nothing within walking distance of the ballpark before or after the game. There are some fast-food joints on Broadway (Whataburger, etc.) and 48th Street, but they're not places where you'll spend a lot of time. So you'll need to go a little afield—but not too far, really—for some great eats.

On Broadway: Boulders on Broadway, where craft beer rules, even to the point where it's used as a central ingredient in the house burger—the Moose Drool beer burger. Yes, the best of Missoula makes an appearance at a Tempe restaurant catering to craft-beer lovers. *Boulders on Broadway, 530 W. Broadway Rd., Tempe; 480/921-9431; bouldersonbroadway.com.*

Keep on the sports theme with Casey Moore's Oyster House, especially on a nice day where you can take advantage of the outdoor seating. Despite the name, this is really a sports bar, and the offerings are pub grub of a higher order—Oysters Rockefeller, cheesesteaks, etc. *Casey Moore's Oyster House, 850 S. Ash Av., Tempe; 480/968-9935; caseymoores.com.*

Built in the old Tempe Railroad Depot, Macayo's Depot Cantina is the Tempe outpost of a popular locally owned chain. The specialty of the house: margaritas, freshly made tortillas, tacos, and enchiladas. Happy Hour (4-7 p.m.) rocks at Macayo's; a few visits to the complimentary buffet will fill you up. Sit out on the deck if you can. *Macayo's Depot Cantina, 300 S. Ash Av., Tempe; 480/ 966-6677; macayo.com.*

If near-authentic Mexican food isn't your thing, you're in luck: downtown Tempe is a short drive away. Tempe is a college town, and as you might expect from a school with a (deserved) party reputation, there are a fair number of establishments in the downtown area for those who imbibe, most centered around Mill Avenue. (The university is located northeast of the training complex; to get there, head east on Broadway Road and then north on Mill Avenue.) At night you can easily wander in and out of the many watering holes and fast-food joints—and they are plentiful, good, and cheap in the Mill Avenue area.

While you can find fine dining in the Arizona State area (House of Tricks, for instance), here are the places a spring-training fan will find most appropriate at the end of a long day in the sun:

Beer fans will want to check out Four Peaks Brewing Co., a brew-pub and restaurant known for its patio, fresh beer (have the Hefeweizen if it's on tap), and good food. Four Peaks features indoor and outdoor seating areas; if you've been out in the sun for a Cubs or Angels spring-training game, don't be a hero—sit inside to avoid further sun exposure. Expect a crowd, even if you're visiting during spring break. (Parking can be a challenge, as your only option is street parking.) While you can get Four Peaks beer at the ballpark, there is a better selection of cheaper quaffs at the original brewpub. *Four Peaks Brewing Co., 1340 E. 8th St., Tempe; 480/303-9967; fourpeaks.com.* Chances are pretty good the Four Peaks beer you had at the ballpark was not made at the brewpub, but rather than at a newer production facility west of Mill Avenue. The Four Peaks Tasting Room is set in an industrial area—fitting for a place devoted to large-scale beer brewing—but it also features some nice touches, including a game area (pool, board games, etc.) and food service via food trucks. *Four Peaks Tasting Room on Wilson, 2401 S. Wilson St., Tempe; 480/ 634-2976; fourpeaks.com.*

At first glance, Rula Bula is an oddity: it looks like an old Wild West saloon with an Irish theme. But go in and you'll see what you assumed to be a Wild West saloon is really an Irish saddlery, taken down from its original location in Waterford, Ireland and then reassembled in Tempe. Yeah, it's a bit odd, but the exotic construction means this is an Irish bar through and through. You can nosh on traditional Irish dishes like fish and chips or purported Irish delicacies like Irish spicy lemon shrimp. *Rula Bula, 401 S. Mill Av., Tempe; 480/929-9500; rulabula.com.*

Another oddity: pasties in Arizona. Pasties are normally associated with Eastern European immigrants—you normally find them in northern Minnesota, Wisconsin, and Michigan's Upper Penin-sula—but the Cornish Pasty Company takes the humble pasty and charges it up with a variety of creative fillings, including lamb vin-daloo and carne adovada. Wash it down with a Hoegaarden White Ale or Mickey's Malt Liquor; both are on the eclectic drink menu. *Cornish Pasty Co., 960 W. University Dr., Tempe; 480/894-6261; cornishpastyco.com.*

Begin your day at Chompie's, the closest thing to an authentic deli in the Valley of the Sun. With bagels, blintzes, latkes, and a full breakfast menu available in the morning, Chompie's is the place to load up before heading to the ballpark. *Chompie's, 1160 E. University, Tempe; 480/557-0700; chompies.com.*

We cover more Tempe attractions in our Chicago Cubs chapter.
Though Sloan Park is technically in Mesa, it's near the boundary
between Mesa and Tempe, and in many ways offers the best of
Tempe while staying with the Cubs' Mesa roots.

Where to Stay

The Buttes (now a Marriott property) is the closest hotel to Tempe
Diablo Stadium, within easy walking distance of the complex. (In
fact, it's not uncommon to see folks hanging out on the road up to
The Buttes to catch a little game action, but the distance is a little
daunting.) It's also one of the more scenic hotels in the Valley of
the Sun: from the freeway it looks like some sort of futuristic neo-
Wrightian extension of the butte. The extension is the Top of the
Rock restaurant, and it offers some great views of the area at sun-
set. *Phoenix Marriott Tempe at The Buttes, 2000 W. Westcourt
Way, Tempe; 602/225-9000; marriott.com.*

Also within walking distance (albeit a long walk on some
unfriendly terrain) is a Homewood Suites. *4750 E Cotton Center
Blvd, Phoenix; 602/470-2100; hilton.com.*

The Angels' official team hotel in 2016 was Extended Stay America (*2165 W. 15th St., Tempe; 480/557-8880; extendedstayamer-
ica.com*).

As the training complex is close to Sky Harbor International Airport, any of the airport hotels (and there are many) would be convenient as well, as would any Phoenix hotel, for that matter.

RV Parks

Apache Palms RV Park (*1836 E. Apache Blvd., Tempe; 480/
966-7399; apachepalmsrvpark.com*) is less than four miles away
from the ballpark.

Flying In

As mentioned, Phoenix Sky Harbor International Airport is close to the training facility. We discuss it in our chapter on Phoenix.

You may also want to consider flying into Tucson and then driving to Phoenix if the fare to Tucson is significantly cheaper. The drive is 117 miles and takes a couple of hours on I-10, but it's a pretty drive if you like desert scenery and getting to the ballpark is convenient because of its location on the south side of the greater Phoenix area.

Spring-Training History: Los Angeles Angels of Anaheim

The major-league Los Angeles Angels began play in the 1961 under the ownership of Gene Autry. (The field at Tempe Diablo Stadium is named for the old singing cowboy.) The team's first spring-training home was Palm Springs, where they played at the Polo Grounds, later renamed Angels Stadium. Angels Stadium still exists, hosting high-school and summer-collegiate baseball.

In 1966, the Angels partially shifted spring training in Holtville, California, and 10 days to two weeks at the four-diamond complex from 1966 through 1979 (splitting time with Palm Springs), before returning on a full-time basis to Palm Springs in 1980. The Angels then reverted back to a split schedule in 1982 and 1983, dividing spring headquarters between Casa Grande, Arizona, and Palm Springs. Between 1984 and 1992, the team trained in Mesa.

In 1993, Angels spring training shifted full-time to Tempe Diablo Stadium. But spring training has been played at this ballpark since 1969: On March 7, a crowd of 1,032 showed up to see the expansion Seattle Pilots defeat the Cleveland Indians, 19-7. Mike Marshall, who would later nab an NL Cy Young Award in 1974 as a reliever with the Los Angeles Dodgers, was the winning pitcher.

INSIDER'S TIP

When spring training first came to Tempe in 1969, the local Chamber of Commerce stepped in to organize everything the Seattle Pilots needed with the formation of the Tempe Diablos, a special events committee. The Tempe Diablos still play an important role in spring training, with over 100 volunteers providing game-day services as ushers, parking-lot attendants, and ticket takers. You'll know them by the straw hats with the distinctive red band. Say hi; volunteer groups like the Tempe Diablos are a vital part of what makes spring training such a unique experience.

Tempe Diablo Stadium was also the site of one of the more surreal periods in MLB history: the final days of the Pilots. Baseball was not exactly a hit in Seattle in 1969 at a former minor-league ballpark with limited capabilities, and during the offseason the owners, led by Pacific Coast League legend Dewey Soriano, tried selling the team before taking refuge in bankruptcy court. With investors led by Allan "Bud" Selig Jr. ready to buy the team, much of the discussion during spring training centered on whether the Pilots would end up back in Seattle or playing at County Stadium as the Milwaukee Brewers. (In fact, AP ran stories showing players in uniforms for both teams.) Finally, late in spring training—March 31, to be exact—a bankruptcy referee signed off on the sale of the Brewers to the Selig group, ending the short history of the Seattle Pilots. (We discuss the situation in more depth in our Milwaukee Brewers chapter.)

The Brewers returned to Tempe Diablo Stadium for spring training again in 1971 and 1972 before shifting operations to Sun City for 1973. Tempe Diablo Stadium would remain empty in springtime until 1977, when the expansion Seattle Mariners set up shop there. The Mariners trained there until spring training 1993, when Gene Autry's California Angels permanently moved to Tempe.

PHOENIX MUNICIPAL STADIUM

QUICK FACTS

- **Capacity**: 8,000
- **Year Opened**: 1965
- **Dimensions**: 345L, 410C, 345R
- **Dugout Location**: First-base side
- **Ticket Line**: 480/727-0000
- **Address**: 5999 E. Van Buren St., Phoenix, AZ 85008-3410
- **Directions**: From the South on I-10: Take exit 143N, turn right on Washington, left on Priest Drive. Phoenix Municipal Stadium is on the corner of Van Buren and Priest. From the West: go on 202, north on Priest Drive. Phoenix Municipal Stadium is on the corner of Van Buren and Priest.

New Life at the Muni

It is a low-key venue, to be sure. But it may be one of the most beautiful venues in college baseball despite being one of the oldest, a ballpark tucked into the foothills of the Papago Park recreation area. What was once a dumpy, old ballpark with uncomfortable bleacher seating and minimalist approach to comfort is now one of our favorite places to catch a baseball game, especially at night.

That old ballpark—Phoenix Municipal Stadium—saw new life in 2015, when the Arizona State University Sun Devils moved from Packard Stadium to nearby Phoenix Muni. It's the second move by a big-time program to a former Arizona spring-training site: as we note in our Tucson chapter, the University of Arizona Wildcats won a national championship after moving into Hi Corbett Field in 2012.

In the case of the Muni, the longtime home to baseball in Phoenix was open after the Oakland Athletics moved to Hohokam Stadium for 2015. The city was looking for a Phoenix Muni tenant (and, quite honestly, to take the ballpark off the city's hands), and the University was looking for a new home after concluding Packard Stadium was not the future of Sun Devils baseball. Packard Stadium was not the most comfortable venue, and with college baseball on the rise, the school was looking to increase ballpark revenues. Fixing up Packard Stadium was deemed to be financially prohibitive—any changes meant meeting ADA standards, not an inexpensive process—and the land underneath the ballpark were worth far more than the ballpark's revenue potential. So the decision was made to move the college program to the far more upscale venue.

While there were some good business reasons for the Oakland Athletics to move to Hohokam Stadium, they did leave behind an attractive venue. A 2004 renovation gave a sense of place to what was once an anonymous facility. There's a strong architectural tradition in Arizona going back to the days of adobe buildings, a style with an emphasis on natural building materials and integration with the buttes that dominate the area. In the case of Phoenix Municipal Stadium, accents made from decorative stones adorn the entryways of the stands, while the general feeling in the concourse echoes the Papago Park surroundings.

The Sun Devils put a lot of effort into making Phoenix Muni their own. Gone are the Athletics colors and signage; new is the yellow and burgundy associated with the ASU program. Gone are the spring training histories found at the back of the grandstand; new are placards celebrating ASU baseball history, including coaches like Bobbly Winkles and venues like Packard Stadium. Gone is the old scoreboard, replaced by a videoboard. Outfield boards detail championships won by the Sun Devils, with a huge board inside listing former players. And with 10 sections of seats down each line covered with tarps, Phoenix Muni now feels like a much more intimate venue.

But the best things about Phoenix Municipal Stadium are still present and enhanced. ASU plays much of its schedule with 6:30 p.m. games, and that's a perfect time to be at the ballpark. Night games at Phoenix Municipal Stadium are a special treat, as the colors off the rock formations beyond center and left field are spectacular. There's always something special about an Arizona sunset, and the reds of the rock formations in the Papago Park recreation area contrast nicely with the yellows and pinks of the night sky. True, the rock formations make a nice backdrop to the action during a day game as well, but at night the colors come out.

Phoenix Municipal Stadium dates back to 1965, built to house spring training, college, and minor-league baseball. This is a return for ASU Sun Devils baseball, as the team played at Phoenix Muni in its early days. (Reggie Jackson hit the first homer for ASU at Phoenix Muni—out of the ballpark, no less.) In those days, this was the edge of the city, with an amusement park next door and little else. All of the seating is located between the foul poles (no outfield grass berm seating here), and it's a mix of chairbacks and backed bleachers. The concessions are located in back of the grandstand and down the left-field line.

ASU baseball at Phoenix Muni was a hit, with the team averaging more than 3,000 fans per game in both 2015 and 2016. With the many night games on the Sun Devils schedule, it's easy to put together your own day-night doubleheader, with an MLB game in the afternoon and an ASU game at night. Highly recommended.

Ballpark History

Phoenix Municipal Stadium was the home of the Triple-A Phoenix Firebirds until 1992, when the team moved to Scottsdale Stadium and played there before the arrival of the Arizona Diamondbacks. It also served as the spring home of the Los Angeles Dodgers for two weeks in 2008, when the Dodgers left Vero Beach early to

play a series in Japan and then spent the remainder of spring training in Phoenix.

The Ballpark Experience

Concessions

Phoenix Municipal Stadium concessions are more limited than
they were in the A's days, but there's still a good selection of hot
dogs, hamburgers, and other ballpark fare. Concession stands are
located down each line and virtually impossible to miss.

And one thing still available at Phoenix Muni: beer. (This is an
off-campus venue with a private concessionaire, after all. No
pesky appearances to keep up with at an on-campus venue.) You'll
encounter the main beer stand when you enter the park, with offerings that include MillerCoors products like Lite and Blue Moon.
The beers are on the craft level, albeit a little expensive. Still:
Magic. Even more magic: Pinot grigio in a can. *In a can.* The
wonders of the modern world.

Parking

There's really no avoiding the $5 charge for parking in a lot across
the ballpark; there is no street parking, and no inclination by the
local businesses to open their lots to baseball fans. Unless you're
at the ballpark early, you'll be parking quite a distance from the
ballpark as well, so bring your walking shoes.

Selfie Spot

When the ballpark was renovated for Sun Devils baseball, a whole
slew of ASU-specific displays were added. Those will be the best
spots for a selfie.

If You Go

What to Do Outside the Ballpark

Though the concession prices at the ballpark are more than reasonable, you may want to grab a bite before or after a game.

Honey Bear's BBQ is a Phoenix institution, scoring a slew of local awards after opening in 1986. It's billed as Tennessee-style ribs and chicken, although the smoking tends to be on the subtle side and the sauce is pretty sweet. There are multiple Honey Bear's locations, but this is the one closest to the ballpark and it's the original location. Don't leave without ordering the sweet-potato pie. *Honey Bear's BBQ, 5012 E. Van Buren St., Phoenix; 602/ 273-9148; honeybearsbbq.com.*

The Stockyards is also a Phoenix institution, albeit for much longer: the original bar has been around since 1889 and the restaurant since 1947. As you can guess from the name, Stockyards is a steak house, but it's also known for its seafood as well. *5001 E.*

Washington St., Phoenix; 602/273-7378; stockyardssteak-
house.com.

If you feel the need to work off some of the BBQ and ballpark
beer, there's Papago Park itself, a 1,200-acre recreational area with
hiking trails, a golf course, fishing ponds, and picnic areas. It also
contains the Phoenix Zoo and the Desert Botanical Garden, which
we discussed in our earlier chapter on Phoenix.

Papago Golf Course is continually one of the top-rated municipal
golf courses in the country. It's not an easy course, carrying a 73.3
championship rating, but it is extremely popular, so reserve your
tee times as early as possible (they can be made up to four days in
advance). *Papago Golf Course, 5595 E. Moreland, Phoenix; 602/
275-8428; papagogolfcourse.net.*

And, of course, you're not too far from Tempe or Scottsdale.
(How close? The ballpark is on the city line, and the office buildings south of the ballpark are technically in Tempe.) Eastbound
Van Buren Street actually turns into Mill Avenue before heading
into downtown Tempe; we describe this party and bar area in our
Los Angeles Angels of Anaheim chapter. From the ballpark, heading north on Galvin, east on McDowell Road, and north on Scottsdale Road will bring you into downtown Scottsdale in practically
no time.

Nearby Hotels

There are many hotels north of the airport that are within two
miles of Phoenix Municipal Stadium. They're virtually all corporate—Marriott, Springhill Suites, Hampton Inn, Doubletree,
Crowne Plaza, Residence Inn—but not necessarily overpriced during spring training. You could do worse than adopting a Phoenix
airport hotel as your base of operations for spring training. We
cover many of these hotels in our introductory chapters.

Nearby RV Resorts

There are no RV resorts in the general area. The closest ones are in Tempe and Scottsdale.

CASINOS, CUBS, AND CASHMAN

Not every spring-training game is played in Florida or Arizona. During the last weekend of spring training, you'll find many teams scattering for points across the country. Some, like the Dodgers/ Angels and A's/Giants, traditionally play a pair of home-and-home games during that last weekend. Others use the occasion to take on a minor-league affiliate or two. Neutral-site games have become a big part of spring training, and in this chapter we'll cover one city with a March tradition of hosting exhibition games: Las Vegas.

The Chicago Cubs have traditionally scheduled exhibition games at Cashman Field, the regular-season home of the Triple-A Las Vegas 51s. Last season the games took place on the final weekend of the season, but in previous years they took place in the middle of the month. Last year the 51s' parent, the New York Mets, took on the Cubs.

Now, as far as ballparks go, 9,334-seat Cashman Field is pretty much strictly utilitarian: Built in 1993, it's an intimate, low-key ballpark. There's some history in the ballpark: when the Oakland A's were forced from the Oakland-Alameda County Coliseum due to an earthquake in 1996, they played their first 16 games at Cashman Field.

For the most part, the park resembles a standard-issue Pacific Coast League facility: all of the seating is between the foul lines, a second level contains press facilities and suites, and there are some decent views of mountains beyond the outfield fence.

But you're not heading to Cashman Field from Chicago or Phoenix or New York City to see the ballpark: you're headed there to see the Cubs, perhaps their competition, or the sports book at Caesar's or Hard Rock. So despite the nature of Cashman Field, you'll probably be considering a visit to Vegas for some baseball and gambling.

By the end of March, there's a good chance of picking up a nasty sunburn at such an open ballpark, so the key to choosing a seat at Cashman Field is finding something in the shade. During a day game, Row L is the first row of the shaded area, with section 9-15 (theater-style seating with drinkholders) under the overhang. Any seat down the line will be open and hot, as metal bleachers dominate the area.

Should you not be able to score seats in the shade, we'd recommend sitting down the line and securing a picnic table in the group area. Your view of the game won't be great—it won't be once you're past the dugouts, in any case—but you'll be able to better socialize with your friends.

If you feel overheated, head to the Plaza Seating area in the grandstand and take advantage of the misting system. *Cashman Field, 850 Las Vegas Boulevard North, Las Vegas; lv51.com. Las Vegas Boulevard is more widely known as The Strip, and virtually everything in Las Vegas is measured by its proximity to the Strip. If you're coming from the south—where most of the glitzy casinos lie—you'll want to follow Las Vegas Boulevard through downtown and past I-515; Cashman Field is a half-mile past the overpass, on the right. Tickets for this game are sold by the 51s: In January or*

*February you can check out the team's website at lv51.com or call
702/943-7200.*

Parking and Transit

There's plenty of parking in the area, but be warned that it's a long
haul from your parking spot to your seat. (Then again, this is
Vegas: there's usually a long hike between the front desk and a
hotel room.) Most of this is due to the unique layout of Cashman
Field; you need to negotiate a large area between the parking lot
and the actual grandstand, followed by a two-story concourse leading to a mezzanine level. From there, you go down to your seat.
The mezzanine level contains most of the concessions.

You can also get to Cashman Field via public transportation. The
301 (Deuce) line runs up and down Las Vegas Boulevard—the
Strip, basically. You'll need to transfer at the downtown Las
Vegas transport center and hop on the northbound 113 bus line. Be
warned it takes about an hour to get from the corner of Flamingo
and Las Vegas Boulevard to the ballpark via bus. Given how
cheap and ubiquitous cabs are in Vegas, you may want to take a
taxi instead. Or, given how cheap rentals can be found, spring for
a car if you're flying into McCarran International Airport.

Where to Stay

If you're headed to Vegas for a downtown baseball game, we'd
recommend staying downtown, as most of the larger joints are
about a mile from Cashman Field. (The walk between downtown
and Cashman Field isn't the most scenic and sometimes a little
creepy, although it's generally not unsafe.) There are some who
swear by downtown Las Vegas—mostly older folks who have
been going there for decades—and there's a certain Rat Pack quality to the area as well. Embrace your inner Dean Martin.

A newcomer on the downtown hotel front is also one of the oldest entries: the Downtown Grand Hotel, formerly the Lady Luck, has been remodeled and rebranded. The Lady Luck had sat empty for several years before it was renovated, and it's now sold as affordable luxury: you can easily find rooms there for $50 (including a $20 resort fee; expect to pay for parking as well) and enjoy a half-mile walk to the ballpark. It's also across the street from the Fremont Street Experience. The vibe is Rat Pack youth, with plenty of pool parties on the rooftop, 17 bar and restaurants, and more. *Downtown Grand Hotel, 206 N. 3rd St., Las Vegas; 855/ 384-7263; downtowngrand.com.*

The Golden Nugget (*129 E. Fremont St., Las Vegas; 866/ 984-6114; goldennugget.com*) is the largest downtown hotel/ casino, and it's also the swankiest. It's been a victim of the cheap hotel rates throughout downtown Las Vegas, which means (depending on how much in advance you reserve) you can find a weekend room there at $109. Good buys include the El Cortez (*600 E. Fremont St.; 702/385-5200; elcortezhotelcasino.com*), the Four Queens (*202 Fremont St.; 800/634-6045; fourqueens.com*), Binion's (*128 E. Fremont St.; 702/382-1600*), and Main Street Station (*850 Las Vegas Blvd. N.; 702-387-1896; mainstreet-casino.com*), which has the advantage of sporting a decent microbrewery, the Triple 7. There's certainly plenty to do if you decide to stay downtown, though you may get tired of the Fremont Street Experience and the endless come-ons to visit the Girls of Glitter Gulch after a day or two.

Downtown Las Vegas is old school, and you'll need to decide whether you want to save some bucks close to the ballpark. Given the huge number of hotel rooms in Vegas and the need for transport to and from the ballpark anyway, there's always the option of staying at one of the huge resort hotels on the Strip—the Flamingo, Bally's, Excalibur, Harrah's, Treasure Island—that don't cost an arm and a leg but still offer plenty of entertainment.

WORLD BASEBALL CLASSIC

Depending on what you expect out of spring training, the World Baseball Classic (WBC) may or may not impact your Cactus League experience. Or you may find that adding a WBC game to your trip may end up being a very positive experience.

The World Baseball Classic is MLB's global tournament, held every four years at a variety of venues around the world, culminating with a championship round in the United States. It's an interesting mix of current MLB players (albeit with relatively few superstars), professionals in foreign leagues (Nippon Professional Baseball, China Baseball League, Chinese Professional Baseball League, Australian Baseball League), independent leagues (American Association, Can-Am League), and national amateur leagues (Cuban National Series).

In 2013, the likes of Nelson Cruz (Dominican Republic), Robinson Cano (Dominican Republic), Yadier and Jose Molina (Puerto Rico), Yulieski Gourriel (Cuba), Carlos Beltran (Puerto Rico), Brett Lawrie (Canada), Justin Morneau (Canada), Pat Venditte (Italy), Jason Grilli (Italy), Yovani Gallardo (Mexico), Joe Mauer (United States), Ben Zobrist (United States) and Giancarlo Stanton (United States) represented their countries in a tournament ultimately won by the Dominican Republic, which defeated Puerto

Rico in the finals. Now, truth be told, you won't see very many superstars taking place in the WBC: most MLB teams fight tooth and nail to keep their best players in camp, especially when it comes to pitchers. You may see a future superstar or two—in 2013, Anthony Rizzo played first for Team Italy, but he was a minor leaguer at the time—and the coaching staffs will feature plenty of former MLB greats. Joe Torre managed the U.S. team in 2013; Jim Leyland will manage the U.S. team in 2017, while Barry Larkin, who coached the 2013 Brazil team, will do the same for the 2017 team.

The first round of games will be held at Seoul's Gocheok Sky Dome, the Tokyo Dome, Marlins Park, and Estadio Charros de Jalisco in Guadalajara. Now, we're guessing most readers of this book will be most interested in the Miami games on March 9-13, featuring play in Pool C (Dominican Republic, United States, Canada and Colombia). That's certainly a glamorous draw for spring-training fans: as noted earlier, the Dominican Republic won the 2013 tournament, and the U.S. team is sure to have some familiar faces.

Spring-training fans may also be interested in the second-round games on March 14-19 at San Diego's Petco Park.

And, of course, Dodger Stadium will host the WBC semifinals and final on March 20-22, 2017. This will be the second time Dodger Stadium has hosted the final two rounds of WBC games, the previous time in 2009.

When the World Baseball Classic launched in 2006, it was partially run as an adjunct to spring training, with games hosted at Champion Stadium, Scottsdale Stadium, and Phoenix's Chase Field, with spring-training games spaced out to accommodate WBC matches. The 2013 tourney also featured a spring-training venue (Salt River Fields). This year's tourney doesn't appear to pose any serious impact on spring training, but you may want to

take a side trip to check out the WBC action in California or
Florida. You are looking at three outstanding venues hosting the
action—and World Baseball Classic games tend to attract enthusiastic fans, to boot.

TUCSON:
PEACE IN
THE VALLEY

Despite the defection of three Cactus League teams—Arizona, Chicago White Sox, and Colorado—in 2010 and 2011, Tucson should still be under consideration for your Arizona spring-training travels. There is one big reason for a trip to Tucson, and that's one of the great old ballparks of baseball, Hi Corbett Field, home of the University of Arizona Wildcats. In addition, Tucson is a lovely place to visit and less than two hours (110 miles) drive from Phoenix.

In many ways Tucson is a smaller version of Phoenix, with many of the same attributes. (Yes, the Tucson tourism folks will hate to see this statement expressed so starkly, but it's true.) Present-day Tucson was founded on August 20, 1775, with a Spanish settlement called Presidio de San Augustin. The structure no longer stands, but the El Presidio neighborhood still exists in downtown Tucson. Tucson has been part of the United States since 1853, except for a brief period when Confederate soldiers invaded the area and declared it Confederate territory.

Tucson is a gorgeous city, where you can count on sunny days and spectacular sunsets. The emphasis in Tucson is on outdoor activities: hikers and walkers will delight in the many offerings of the city, while nature lovers will enjoy spending time in the Sonoran

Desert. And Tucson is a university town, with all the life and
excitement that it entails.

Even though Tucson is in the midst of the desert, you'll want to
pack for cooler weather for a spring-training trip. The average
March high is 75 (but feels much warmer if you're from the north
and not used to a warm spring sun), but lows dip down to 45.
There's a smattering of rain during the month as well.

There are two major ballparks in Tucson: Hi Corbett Field, the historic home of the University of Arizona Wildcats, and Kino Stadium, which in the past several years has hosted MLB exhibitions.
Both hosted spring training for decades.

Hi Corbett Field: A Classic Oasis

No doubt about it: Hi Corbett Field is a classic old ballpark worth
the drive from Phoenix. Much of the ballpark dates back to the
1930s, even though it's been extensively renovated several times
during the years—most recently in 1999, when a team store and a
ticket office were added, and in 1997, when a $3.77 million reno-
vation yielded new seating and expanded the clubhouses. Gone are
the days when kids sat atop the adobe home-run wall, but it's hard
not to imagine them hanging out and cheering on their favorite
Cleveland Indians player back in the day.

Hi Corbett Field holds 8,665, but only 4,000 of these seats provide
good views of the field—which isn't an issue for most University
of Arizona Wildcat games. The box seats behind home plate are a
great value. The grandstand's pitch is severe enough to allow the
seats in the back to be close to the action, and these seats are the
closest to the concessions. You'll want to stick to this middle
grandstand on a hot day: The metal bleachers are both uncomfortable and angled toward the outfield.

The old ballpark received new life in 2012 when the University of

Arizona Wildcats shifted baseball operations there. What resulted was a storybook season: attendance at Wildcats games soared (the team is now one of the best draws in the nation), and the team won the College World Series. The fans have kept coming out ever since. A game at Hi Corbett Field is well worth the effort.

Parking is a bonus at Hi Corbett: it's free, provided you show up early enough to snare one of the spots in the small parking lot.

INSIDER'S TIP
There is plenty of parking on East Camino Campestre, adjacent to what used to be the minor-league complex for the Colorado Rockies.

The ballpark is in an idyllic section of Tucson, on the fringes of a city park and golf course. You're far away from the city when you're watching the Wildcats in action, even though you're physically in a very busy part of town. (You'll discover that fact when you drive down Broadway to get to the ballpark.)

And it certainly is scenic. There is a distinct Southwestern motif to Hi Corbett Field, something that fits right into the Tucson ethos. Adobe has always been part of the spring vibe here: the original configuration had an adobe outfield wall where fans sat and watched the games for free. Add a clock tower to the mix, and Hi Corbett is one of the prettiest ballparks in college baseball.

The ballpark is named for Hiram Steven "Hi" Corbett, the president of the Tucson Baseball Commission and the man who worked with Bill Veeck to bring the Cleveland Indians to town.

INSIDER'S TIP
Bring your sunscreen. There's precious little seating not in direct sunlight.

Hi Corbett Field, 3400 E. Camino Campestre, Tucson; arizonawildcats.com. From I-10, exit at Broadway, head east and then turn

*right on Randolph Way. Hi Corbett is located on the right-hand
side. There are signs pointing the way.*

Ballpark History

Hi Corbett Field opened in 1928 as Randolph Municipal Baseball
Park, the home of the minor-league Class D Tucson Waddies from
the original Arizona State League. (Some of those Arizona State
League teams had interesting names, including the Tucson Missions, Lizards, and Cowboys). Later on, the ballpark housed the
Tucson Toros of the Triple-A Pacific Coast League, and the University of Arizona played night games there as well in the 1960s.
The Cleveland Indians trained at Hi Corbett Field from 1947
through 1992 thanks to owner Bill Veeck, who wanted the team
close to his Arizona ranch. The Colorado Rockies trained there
from 1993 through 2010.

If You Go

What to Do Outside the Ballpark

Hi Corbett is part of a larger complex that includes Randolph
Municipal Golf Course, Gene Reid Park, and the Reid Park Zoo.
Reid Park Zoo features over 400 animals, including anteaters and
polar bears. It has also one of the more active breeding programs,
with white rhinoceroses and ruffed lemurs on display. *Reid Park
Zoo, 1030 S. Randolph Way, Tucson; 520/881-4753; tucson-
zoo.org. Adults, $9; seniors, $7; children (2-14), $5.*

Randolph Municipal Golf Course contains two courses. If you can
handle the distance (7,000 yards from the championship tees,
6,500 yards from the regular tees), Randolph North is gorgeous;
the fairways are lined with eucalyptus trees and palms, and the
mountains make a lovely backdrop. Randolph Dell Urich is shorter
(5,800 yards from the regular tees) and easier to walk, making it

the more popular course. *Randolph Municipal Golf Course, 600 S. Alvernon Way, Tucson; 520/791-4161; tucsoncitygolf.com.*

Where to Stay

There are a few excellent hotels within a mile or so of the ballpark:

- Doubletree Hotel Tucson—Reid Park, 445 S. Alvernon Way, Tucson; 520/881-4200; *doubletree.com.*
- La Quinta Inn & Suites Tucson—Reid Park, 102 N. Alvernon Way, Tucson; 520/795-0330; *lq.com.*
- Lodge on the Desert, 306 N. Alvernon Way, Tucson; 520/325-3366, 800/456-5634; *lodgeonthedesert.com.* This hotel dates back to 1936 and was designed in a hacienda style, complete with tile-covered patios and fireplaces.

In addition, there is a varied selection of hotels near the University of Arizona and downtown Tucson, each of which is less than five miles away.

RV Parks

There are a host of RV parks in the Tucson area. Most of them are on the outskirts of town (the better to view the Sonoran Desert, of course) and geared more toward long-term snowbirds. The closest is Pima Swan RV Park (*4615 E. Pima St., Tucson; 520-881-4022; pimaswanrvpark.com*), which is just under four miles from the ballpark.

Kino Stadium: Where the Major Leaguers Played

Kino Stadium (the former Tucson Electric Park) doesn't host spring training any longer, and it recently lost its last primary ten-

ant, as the Pacific Coast League's Tucson Padres moved to El
Paso for the 2014 season.

Kino Stadium is a basic suburban facility, with easy freeway
access. After parking in the adjoining lot, you enter Kino Stadium
at ground level and look down to the action from a concourse
level. The playing field is below grade. The main grandstand area
features theater-style seats, while there are two levels of bleachers
down each line.

The outfield area is noteworthy in that there's not a single bleacher
seat; instead, the designers wisely put in grassy areas on both sides
of a concession area in dead-center field. It's a great area for families to throw down a blanket—the kids can run around and play
catch, while the adults get a great view of the action. The bullpens
are in front of the center-field concession stand, and you can look
down at them from the outfield grass. A concourse rings the entire
playing field, so you can wander throughout the stadium during
the course of a game.

When the Diamondbacks and White Sox left Kino Stadium, city
and Pima County officials were determined to bring back MLB
spring training and pursued every lead under the sun. But with
Cactus League spring training centralized in Phoenix and no team
looking to move away, it looks like springtime in Tucson means
soccer, both pro and amateur—and given the money youth soccer
brings into the area, that's not the worst of outcomes.

*Kino Stadium, 2500 E. Ajo Way, Tucson. From I-10 North: Take
exit 263B and turn right on Ajo Way. The ballpark will be on your
right. From I-10 South: Take exit 263 and turn right on Ajo Way.
The ballpark will be on your right.*

If You Go

Where to Stay

Kino Stadium is within four miles of both the airport and downtown Tucson, which means that you can easily stay at one of the many chains represented in both locales and then have a short commute to the ballpark.

The airport hotels actually begin about a mile from the ballpark, so you can stay there and have easy access to the action. But Tucson is not the sort of community where you want to do a lot of walking: there's nothing within easy pedestrian distance of the ballpark (a Quality Inn is technically about a mile from the ballpark, but it's not an easy walk), so a car rental will be necessary for a visit unless you drive down from Phoenix.

Tucson Activities

You won't spend all your time at the ballpark, so here's a selection of other activities in the area.

Located west of downtown, Sentinel Peak (sometime called "A" Mountain because of the University of Arizona "A" at the peak) was inhabited for thousands of years by the Hohokam Indians. Hohokam, which means "the vanished ones," farmed the area, but then inexplicably disappeared, replaced by other Native American tribes. (It's the same Hohokam tribe honored by volunteers at the spring home of the Oakland Athletics.) Today you can drive to the top of the mountain and see some great views of the entire Tucson basin. *Sentinel Peak, Sentinel Peak Road.*

In 1692, Father Eusebio Francisco Kino made the first of his many trips to the area. Kino, an Italian missionary for the Spanish church, established a string of missions in Arizona and Sonora, with the most famous being San Xavier del Bac Mission, the

"White Dove of the Desert," founded in 1694. It didn't start out as a white structure when constructed in 1797, but a 1900s renovation led to the repainting of the exterior in brilliant white, which is stunning in the desert sun. It still features regular masses as a Catholic parish. *San Xavier del Bac Mission, 1950 W. San Xavier Rd., Tucson; 520/294-2624; sanxaviermission.org.*

The city of Tucson runs five municipal courses; you can reserve tee times at any of them by calling 888/214-8537 or 520/ 791-GOLF (4653) or *tucsoncitygolf.com.* There is also an abundance of public and private courses throughout the area; check out rates and listings at *visitTucson.org.*

The Spanish Missionary style dominates the local architecture. To see a good selection of historic buildings of that era, hit downtown Tucson. Some of the best examples are government buildings, like the State Building (416 W. Congress St.) and the Pima County Courthouse (15 N. Church Av.), while others formerly were private residences, like the Manning House (450 W. Paseo Redondo) and the Stevens House (150 N. Main Av.).

Tombstone is the site of the legendary gunfight at OK Corral, where the Earps and Doc Holliday fought the Clantons and McLaurys. Today Tombstone, located south of Tucson on state Highway 80, is preserved with a downtown historic district that features many original buildings, stagecoach rides, and daily reenactments of the famous gunfight. Located south of town: Boothill Graveyard, where many of the local gunslingers were laid to rest. *OK Corral, Tombstone; 520/457-3456, 888/457-3929; ok-corral.com.*

Tucson Dining

The home of Southwestern cuisine, Tucson is known as a town with great food. We have some favorites.

Food-truck culture has hit Tucson hard, and why not? The trucks can run 12 months a year, there's an abundance of millennials eager to make their mark on food culture, and the economics are compelling. You'll find some of the better Southwestern cuisine served out of one of the many food trucks operating in the university area.

If you need a NCAA basketball tournament fix in the midst of your visit, a traditional sports bar is the Bob Dobbs Bar & Grill, a neighborhood joint near the University of Arizona campus where the beer is cold, the burgers are huge, and the sound system is unobtrusive. The Bob Burger is a half-pounder flavored with garlic and Worcestershire sauce. And yes, the bar was originally named for J.R. "Bob" Dobbs, the founder of the Church of the Subgenius: Give me slack, or give me food, or kill me. *Bob Dobbs Bar & Grill, 2501 E. 6th St., Tucson; 520/325-3767; bobdobbs.net.*

For pure Mexican food, there is the El Charro Café, with two locations: downtown and on the east side of Tucson. El Charro Café is touted as being the oldest Mexican restaurant in continual operation by the same family in America, dating back to 1922. Try the Carne Seca Beef. *El Charro Café downtown, 311 N. Court Av.; 520/622-1922; elcharrocafe.com.*

The Fourth Avenue stretch near the University of Arizona features a variety of eateries and bars at a wide range of prices. Caruso's has been serving inexpensive Italian food to UA students since 1938, with three generations of the Zagona family at the helm. Pasta and lots of it dominate the menu. Sit outside on the patio if you can. *Caruso's, 434 N. 4th Av., Tucson; 520/624-5765; carusositalian.com.*

Finally, there is an abundance of microbreweries in the area. Our favorite is one of the newest: Ten Fifty-Five Brewing, a purposely small-scale operation focusing on small batches and fresh ingredients. The Lazy Duck Wheat is perfect on a hot afternoon; the Leap Pale Ale is the flagship. You can find their beers throughout the Tucson area, but a trip to the brewery is recommended—especially on a Saturday, when the food trucks descend. *Ten Fifty-Five Brewing, 3810 E. 44th St., Suite 315, Tucson; 520/461-8073; 1055brewing.com.*

Where to Stay

Tucson hotels tend to be concentrated in downtown, near the University, and adjoining the airport. For those attending baseball games, the downtown and airport areas offer the easiest access to the ballparks. Tucson is the second-largest city in Arizona, but it doesn't have an abundance of hotel rooms, so you may find your selections to be somewhat limited. However, spring break is not a huge event in Tucson, so it's not difficult to find a hotel in your price range.

Since you probably won't be staying near the ballpark, we do have a recommendation if you're in search of interesting lodgings. Perhaps the most unique hotel in Tucson is the Hotel Congress, originally built in 1919 to serve passengers on the Southern Pacific Line. The rooms are inexpensive—$109 for a king suite, $89 for a single—and are outfitted with vintage fixtures like wrought-iron beds and antique radios. It's not for everyone (you won't be pampered by today's standards, and forget entertaining the kids with Cartoon Network) and the noise from downstairs can be loud (especially when a band is playing), but for those in search of a unique travel experience, Hotel Congress rocks.

Inside the lobby of the Hotel Congress is the Cup Café and the Tap Room. The Cup Café isn't as old as the rest of the hotel (it dates back to 1990), but it's worth a visit even if you're not staying in the hotel. The dining theme at dinner is a fusion of Southwestern, Asian, Mediterranean, and more; sit at the bar for a unique experience. Better yet: breakfast, where $14 gets you a filling meal. An old cowboy bar, the Tap Room has been open continuously since 1919, complete with paintings from noted cowboy artist Pete Martinez. Check out the jukebox as well. *Hotel Congress, 311 E. Congress St., Tucson; 520/622-8848, 800/722-8848; hotelcongress.com.*

Transportation

You'll need a car to see most of the sights in Tucson. Although there is public transportation in the form of Sun Tran (*suntran.com*), Tucson is a sprawling metropolitan area. If you're not driving in, you can rent a car at the airport: all the major car-rental companies are located either inside the terminal or at a nearby facility.

Flying In

Tucson International Airport is located on the south side of town, near Kino Stadium. Most major airlines (Alaska Airlines, American, Delta, Southwest, and United) fly into Tucson, although there are a limited number of nonstop flights. It's also a rather fetching airport: it was built in 1963 and the main terminal still has a classic Southwest façade. *Tucson International Airport, 7005 S. Plumer Av., Tucson; 520/573-8100; tucsonairport.org.*

ALSO FROM AUGUST PUBLICATIONS

The Complete Guide to Spring Training 2017 / Florida

The Baseball Thesaurus

The Football Thesaurus

Cradle of the Game: North Carolina Baseball Past and Present

Never a Bad Game: 50 Years of the Southern League

Raye of Light: Jimmy Raye, Duffy Daugherty, The Integration of College Football, and the 1965-1966 Michigan State Spartans

Goodfellows: The Champions of St. Ambrose

Available from Amazon, Barnes & Noble, and augustpublications.com!